A CULTURAL TRADITIONS DIRECTORY
FOR NORTHERN IRELAND

Compiled by Maurna Crozier and Nicholas Sanders

Institute of Irish Studies

CONTENTS

PREFACE

During the last few years, the upsurge of interest in cultural traditions and heritage has been evident in the enthusiasm of the local history movement, in community-initiated exhibitions, plays and publications, and in the introduction of cultural heritage educational material in our schools. In response to this, there has been a tremendous increase in the number of books, films and educational packs addressing a wide range of topics relating to the history, traditions, and social and environmental context of Northern Ireland. This Cultural Traditions Directory is a first attempt to gather such information into one volume of reference.

Some of the organizations whose materials are listed were exhibitors at the Cultural Traditions Resources Fair held in September 1991 in Belfast and it was the frequent requests for such a volume, from the many visitors to the fair, which confirmed the need for the Directory. Strenuous attempts have been made, through the local and national press and broadcasting stations, to bring the Directory to the attention of all potential contributors and the inclusion of material has been determined principally by the response to this initiative. Although every effort has been made to make it as inclusive as possible, it is inevitable that some groups or individuals may not have heard of the plans for the publication and so are not represented. It is hoped that there may be an up-dated publication sometime in the future and new contributions could then be added. The inclusion here of a 'Forthcoming' category is intended not only to give an indication of work in hand, but also to show where there are gaps which authors and publishers may wish to address.

The compilers of the Directory would like to thank all those involved in preparing lists of resources, and especially Fiona Murray who collated and organised much of the material. Particular thanks are due to the Cultural Traditions Group and the Community Relations Council for recognising and responding to the need for such a publication, and for supporting it financially.

Maurna Crozier
January 1992

ADARE PRESS

Doreen McBride, 'White Gables', Ballymoney Hill, Banbridge, Co Down BT32 4DR.
Tel: 082 06 23782.

Independent publisher of books of Irish interest.

Books:

Stand Up and Tell Them; Liz Weir (ed); 1991; £4.95.
>   Traditional style recitations by three Northern Ireland writers, offering valuable social comment in a humorous way.

We Are Our Past; Doreen McBride; 1990; £4.95.
>   Customs, folklore and beliefs, fairies, banshees, famine and emigration are described in simple language, supported by black and white photographs and line drawings.

What They Did With Plants; Doreen McBride; 1991; £4.95.
>   How plants have been used for linen and putty manufacture, for dyes, country cures and food.

APPLETREE PRESS

Appletree Press Ltd, 7 James Street South, Belfast BT2 8DN. Tel: 0232 243074.

Belfast based publisher of a wide range of books, many of which are of great value for cultural heritage studies.

Books:

Belfast: the Making of the City; J C Beckett et al; £6.95.

Dictionary of Irish Place Names; Adrian Room; £9.95/£4.95.

Dressed to Kill: Cartoonists & the Northern Ireland Conflict; John Darby; £2.95.

Famous Irish Lives; Martin Wallace; £3.99.

Irish Country Cures; Patrick Logan; £5.95.

Irish Myth & Legend; Ronan Coghlan; £3.99.

Irish Place Names; P W Joyce; £3.99.

Irish Traditional Music; Ciaran Carson; £3.99.

John Pepper's Ulster Phrase Book; illustrated by Ralph Dobson; £2.95.

John Pepper's Ulster-English Dictionary; illustrated by Rowel Friers; £2.95.

My Lady of the Chimney Corner; Alexander Irvine; £4.95.
    Celebrated account of a Co Antrim childhood.

Northern Ireland: Background to the Conflict; John Darby (ed); £12.00/£5.95.

One Potato, Two Potato; Bernagh Brims (ed); £2.99.
    Selection of children's stories from the BBC schools series of the same name.

One Potato, Two Potato, Three Potato, Four; Bernagh Brims (ed); £2.99.
    Second selection of stories from the BBC series.

People of Ireland; Patrick Loughrey (ed); £14.95/£8.95.

Pocket Tin Whistle Tutor; Francis McPeake; £3.99.

Short History of Ireland; Martin Wallace; £3.99.

Standing Stones & Other Monuments of Early Ireland; Kenneth McNally; £6.99.

Times of Our Lives; Walter Love; £6.99.
    Six Ulster men and women recall experiences from Belfast, Derry and the Ulster countryside.

Tracing Your Irish Roots; Christine Kinealy; £3.99.

Trouble Free!; Rowel Friers; £3.50.
    Cartoons.

Ulster Trivia Quiz; Robert Kirk; £2.50.

Ulster's Uncertain Defenders: Loyalists & the Northern Ireland Conflict; Sarah
    Nelson; £12.00/£5.95.

Worlds Apart: Segregated Schools in Northern Ireland; Dominic Murray;
    £5.95.

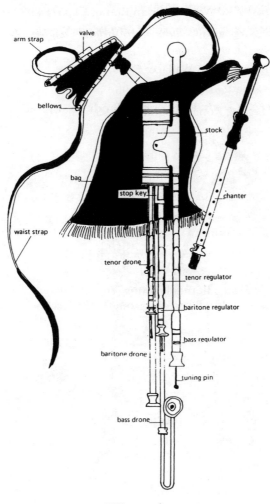

Uilleann pipes

ARMAGH COUNTY MUSEUM

Armagh County Museum, The Mall East, Armagh BT61 9BE. Tel: 0861 524052.

The main concerns of the Museum are the promotion of an awareness of the rich local history and architectural heritage of Armagh and its importance as an ecclesiastical centre.

Books:

Fateful Day; Damien Woods; 1989.

Historical Photographs of the Primatial City; Roger Weatherup; 1990.

Way to the Stars; Mart de Groot; 1990.

Video:

Armagh: One Fair County; Fast Forward Productions; 1991.

From volume IV *Mulloghbawn Folklore and Historical Society*

ARMAGH PIPERS' CLUB

Armagh Pipers' Club, 14 Victoria Street, Armagh BT61 9DT.

The club is involved in the teaching and publication of traditional music.

Tutor Books:

Fifty Reels; Brian & Eithne Vallely; 1982.

Fifty Simple Tunes for the Tin Whistle; Brian & Eithne Vallely; 1978.
  Includes cassette.

Learn to Play the Fiddle; Brian & Eithne Vallely; 1976.

Learn to Play the Tin Whistle (Pts 1–3); Brian & Eithne Vallely; 1972 &
  1973.

Learn to Play the Uillean Pipes; Brian & Eithne Vallely; 1975.

Second Fifty Tunes; Brian & Eithne Vallely; 1992.
  Tunes for playing on tin whistle, fiddle, Uillean pipes, concertina,
  flute, banjo etc.

Sing a Song & Play It (Pts 1-3); Brian & Eithne Vallely; 1974.
  Aimed at 7–14 year olds; a teachers' book is also available and
  includes all three parts.

From *Sing a Song & Play it* (Armagh Pipers' Club)

ARTS COUNCIL OF NORTHERN IRELAND

Arts Council of Northern Ireland, Arts Council Gallery, Bedford Street, Belfast BT2 7FD.
Tel: 0232 321402.

Through its cultural traditions allocation, the Council funds a number of programmes which are extensions of its normal practice. It has also produced several monographs and exhibition catalogues, including biographical details of Irish artists, of which a list is available. The Arts Council Gallery has a large selection of art video films, including Irish artists, which may be viewed there at any time.

Books:

Causeway: the Arts in Ulster; Michael Longley (ed); £0.50.
    Comprehensive survey of the arts, from painting and sculpture to traditional music.

Here is a Health; Sean Corcoran.
    Traditional songs and dance music, collected in Co Fermanagh.

Planter & the Gael; John Hewitt & John Montague; £0.50.
    Poetry collection.

Children's Books:

Big Striped Golfing Umbrella; Mebh McGuckian (ed) & Anne Carlisle (illus); 1985.
    Poems by young people from Northern Ireland.

Tale to Tell; Martin Waddell (ed); 1982.
    Stories by young people from Northern Ireland.

Under the Moon, Over the Stars; Michael Longley (ed); 1971.
    Young people's writing from Ulster.

Programmes:

Mumming.
    Support for the Armagh Rhymers and other groups.

Publishing.
    A series of pamphlets documenting various aspects of traditional music and dance, as practised by both communities in Northern Ireland.

Schools.
Performances and demonstrations in schools by local traditional musicians.

Set dancing.
Performances, workshops and seminars.

Storytelling.
Sessions at a variety of venues.

Slide Pack:

Modern Irish Landscape Painting; £2.50.
Slides of work and biographical notes on artists.

Visual Arts Services to Education:

Artists in schools scheme.

Belfast Print Workshop.

Gallery services.

Mural scheme.

Sculpture Park.

Touring exhibitions.

BBC NORTHERN IRELAND

BBC Education, Broadcasting House, Ormeau Avenue, Belfast
BT2 8HQ.
Tel: 0232 338435.

In seeking to provide audio and visual resources not available
from other sources, the wide range of output on BBC radio and
television offers teachers and pupils, in both primary and
secondary schools, materials about past and present life on the
island of Ireland.

Teachers' Notes (Primary):

One Potato, Two Potato.

Primary Irish.

Primary Music.

Today & Yesterday in Northern Ireland.

Ulster in Focus.

Teachers' Notes (Secondary):

Explorations: Irish Writing.

Geography Ireland.

Irish History: Perspectives.

Study Ireland: History.

BELFAST FILM WORKSHOP

Belfast Film Workshop, 37 Queen Street, Belfast BT1 6EA.
Tel: 0232 326661.

The workshop considers the audio-visual educational process of
film/video production to be an important element in
establishing a facility to promote mutual understanding within
the cultural traditions field and a celebration of personal and
community growth. The workshop facilitates such a process
through the co-operative production of quality film, video,
animation and computer graphics work.

Videos:

Life & Times of Traditional Musical Instruments; Alastair Herron; 1991
    onwards; [ages 12–16].
    Six, ten minute video programmes with accompanying texts.

From *Learn to play the fiddle* (Armagh Pipers' Club)

BIG TELLY THEATRE COMPANY

Bernie McGill, Administrator, Flowerfield Arts Centre, Portstewart, Co Londonderry BT55 7JG.
Tel: 026 58 33959.

The primary aim of the company is to research and write plays about Northern Ireland people, drawing inspiration from their characteristics rather than the political situation. The objective is achieved through a programme of workshops and seminars on different aspects of social and theatrical communication.

Own Plays:

Crumbs!; 1989.

Little Lucy's Magic Box; 1990.

Onions Make You Cry; 1988.

Reconstruction of Dunluce Castle (Crown copyright)

BLACKSTAFF PRESS

The Blackstaff Press, 3 Galway Park, Dundonald, Belfast
BT16 0AN.
Tel: 0232 487161. Fax: 0232 489552.

Award-winning Belfast publisher with wide range of
professionally presented and actively marketed books covering
all aspects of Northern Ireland, from history to poetry and art.

Books:

Across the Narrow Sea; Sam Hanna Bell; £4.95.

Aran Islands; J M Synge; £9.95.

As I Roved Out; Cathal O'Byrne; £12.95.

At Points of Need; Eric Gallagher; £7.95.

Biting at the Grave; Padraig O'Malley; £9.95.

Blitz; Brian Barton; £12.95.

Book of Ulster Surnames; Robert Bell; £6.95.

Catch Yerself On; John Pepper; £3.95.

Chronicle of Irish Saints; Laurence Flanagan; £12.95.

December Bride; Sam Hanna Bell; £4.99.

Faces at the Fair; Stanley Matchett; £0.35.

Frontier Town; Tony Canavan; £10.95.

Gaelic Games Quiz Book; Padraig Coyle; £1.50.

Hell or Connaught; Peter Berresford Ellis; £5.95.

Hollow Ball; Sam Hanna Bell; £4.95.

House of Children; Joyce Cary; £4.95.

Images of Belfast; Robert Johnstone and Bill Kirk; £12.50.

Irish Reciter; Niall Toibin; £4.95.

Kings in Conflict; W A Maguire (ed); £14.95.

Kites in Spring; John Hewitt; £1.50.

Life & Times of Mary Ann McCracken; Mary McNeill; £4.95.

Livin' in Drumlister; W F Marshall; £4.95.

Long Embrace; Frank Ormsby (ed); £7.95.

Meaning of Irish Place Names; James O'Connell; £2.95.

Middle of My Journey; John Boyd; £5.95.

Mountain Year; Michael J Murphy; £0.50.

New Younger Irish Poets; Gerald Dawe (ed); £6.95.

No Surrender; Robert Harbinson; £4.50.

Ould Orange Flute; Traditional; £0.95.

Picking up the Linen Threads; Betty Messenger; £2.50.

Poets from the North of Ireland; Frank Ormsby (ed); £9.95.

Protegé; Robert Harbinson; £4.50.

Pure Drop; John Killen (ed); £3.95.

Quare Geg; John Pepper; £3.95.

Red is the Port Light; Joseph Tomelty; £3.95.

Report on the Loss of the SS Titanic; (Official Government Enquiry); £12.95.

Road to the Somme; Philip Orr; £9.95.

See Me, See Her?; John Pepper; £3.95.

Selected John Hewitt; Alan Warner (ed); £4.95.

Shipbuilders to the World; Michael Moss and John R Hume; £25.00.

Siege City; Brian Lacy; £11.95.

Thine in Storm & Calm; Amanda McKittrick Ros; £0.50.

Titanic: a Survivor's Story; Archibald Gracie; £5.95.

Told in Gath; Max Wright; £5.95.

Ulster Joke Book; Geoff Hill; £2.95.

Ulster Reciter; Joe McPartland; £3.95.

Up Spake the Cabin Boy; Robert Harbinson; £4.50.

What a Thing to Say; John Pepper; £3.95.

CARRICKFERGUS & DISTRICT HISTORICAL SOCIETY

Mrs Helen Rankin, Secretary, Carrickfergus & District Historical Society, 13 Churchill Drive, Carrickfergus, Co Antrim BT38 7LH. Tel: 096 03 62784.

The Society collects and publishes information on the history and personalities of the Carrickfergus area.

Book:

Curious in Everything: the Career of Arthur Dobbs of Carrickfergus (1689–1765); Helen Rankin & Charles Nelson (eds); £3.00.

Journal:

Volumes 1–5; 1985–89.

Volume 6; in prep.

CARRICKFERGUS GASWORKS PRESERVATION SOCIETY

The Carrickfergus Gasworks Preservation Society Ltd,
75 Fernagh Drive, Newtownabbey, Co Antrim BT37 0BH.

The Society's objective is to preserve the Carrickfergus gasworks
and open it to the public as a museum of the gas industry. Its
activities include study of the local industrial heritage and
research of the social impact of the mains gas supply and coal gas
by–products.

Book:

Like a Phoenix From the Flames: Carrickfergus Gasworks; Fred Hamond;
1989.

Video:

Last Retort: Carrickfergus Gasworks Appeal; Alan Soutar; 1990.

Forthcoming:

Carrickfergus Gas Company Limited: the First Ten Years; Denis Mayne.

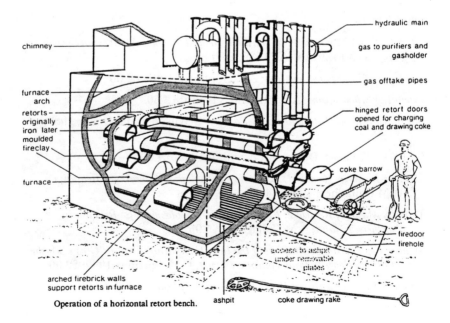

Operation of a horizontal retort bench.

CENTRE FOR THE STUDY OF CONFLICT

Pat Shortt, Centre for the Study of Conflict, University of Ulster, Coleraine, Co Londonderry BT52 1SA.
Tel: 0265 44141. Fax: 0265 40917.

The Centre aims to promote and encourage research on the community conflict in Ireland; to provide a forum for cross-disciplinary and comparative studies; to make an informed and impartial contribution to the public discussion of the conflict; to develop a general and theoretical understanding of conflict from a strong empirical base; to relate research findings to policy and practice; and to develop a comparative programme of research on ethnic conflict on an international basis. These aims are achieved by encouraging the growth of an academic community involved in conflict research and supporting it through seminars, publications, visiting scholars and liaison with other institutions.

Occasional Papers:

Community Conflict: Policy & Possibilities; Donald Horowitz; 1990.

Conflict Research; Maurice Hayes; 1990.

Reports:

Education and Community in Northern Ireland: Schools Apart? and Schools Together?; J Darby et al; 1989; £5.00.

Employment in Divided Societies; A C Hepburn; 1981; £2.00.

Extending School Links; A Smith and S Dunn; £3.50.

Integrated Schools: Information for Parents; D Wilson and S Dunn; 1989; £1.95.

Inter School Links; S Dunn and A Smith; 1989; £4.00.

Majority Minority Review 1: Education & Religion in Northern Ireland; A M Gallagher; 1989; £4.95.

Majority Minority Review 2: Employment, Unemployment & Religion in Northern Ireland; A M Gallagher; £5.95.

Making Ripples: an Evaluation of the Inter-Community Contact Grant Scheme of the Northern Ireland Voluntary Trust; C McCartney; 1990; £2.00.

Northern Ireland Centre in Brussels: a Feasibility Study; 1990; £2.00.

Peace Building in a Political Impasse: Cross-Border Links in Ireland; D Murray and J O'Neill; £3.00.

Role of the Churches; D Morrow; £6.00.

Violence & Communities; A Hamilton et al; £4.00.

The wooden bridge, Derry, from *Across the Foyle* (Guildhall Press)

CLASSIC TRAX

Ms F Caldbeck, Classic Trax BCR, Russell Court, Lisburn Road, Belfast BT9 6JX.
Tel: 0232 438500.

Belfast Community Radio broadcasts a wide range of music and speech material, including 'Airneal', a bi-lingual Irish language programme, and 'Belfast Matters' which covers issues, events and happenings in the greater Belfast area.

THE MUSICAL SCRIBE
Edward Bunting (1773-1843)
From *Lives* (Poolbeg)

CLEGNAGH PUBLISHING

Clegnagh Publishing, Clegnagh House, Armoy, Ballymoney, Co Antrim BT53 8UB.
Tel: 026 57 51625.

Clegnagh is principally concerned with the publication of archaeological and literary material which relates to Irish beliefs and culture but also organises lectures, study tours and conferences to demonstrate how archaeological evidence can demonstrate the strong similarities between apparently disparate traditions.

Books:

Forgotten Places of the North Coast; J D C Marshall; 1991; £7.50.

Forgotten Poems of the North Coast; Jon Marshall; 1991; £7.50.

Forthcoming:

Dictionary of Irish Antiquities; J D C Marshall; 11/92.

Greek Vases & Empty Vessels; Jon Marshall; 11/92.

International Bronze Age of Ireland; J D C Marshall; 11/92.

Clegnagh House

COMMUNITY RELATIONS COUNCIL

Community Relations Council, 6 Murray Street, Belfast
BT1 6DN.
Tel: 0232 439953. Fax: 0232 235208.

The Council seeks to promote greater tolerance and mutual
understanding between the communities in Northern Ireland.
Fostering an appreciation and acceptance of cultural diversity is
an important part of this work.

Booklet:

Whither Cultural Diversity? ; Maurice Hayes.
> Publication of speech delivered by the Chairman of the Cultural
> Traditions Group of the Community Relations Council to the
> MSSc Irish Studies Forum at the Queen's University of Belfast in
> November 1990.

Forthcoming Journal:

Cultural Traditions; 1992.

From *Varieties of Irishness* (Institute of Irish Studies)

CRAIGAVON HISTORICAL SOCIETY

Mr D B Cassells, Honorary Secretary, Craigavon Historical Society, 2 Cherryville Park, Lurgan, Co Armagh BT66 7BA. Tel: 0762 325329.

The Society records the local history of the greater Craigavon area and holds extensive collections of photographs and of farm machinery and implements. It publishes original research on local places, characters, traditions, trades, occupations and industries, and organises a local history competition for schools.

Journal:

Review; bi-annually.

The Forge, from *A journey into the past* (Ulster American Folk Park)

DOE/HISTORIC MONUMENTS & BUILDINGS BRANCH

Conservation Service, Historic Monuments & Buildings Branch, Department of the Environment, 5–33 Hill Street, Belfast BT1 2LA.
Tel: 0232 235000.

The Historic Monuments & Buildings Branch protects historic sites and monuments in Northern Ireland for present and future generations and promotes interest in them.

Books:

Ballycopeland Windmill Souvenir Book; £0.50.

Carrickfergus Castle; £5.90.

Celtic Monasticism; £5.95.

Excavations at Mountsandel; £13.50.

Finding & Minding, 1983–86; £2.70.

Finding & Minding, 1986–89; £2.90.

Historic Monuments of Northern Ireland; £4.90.

Inch Abbey: a Site Based Study; £1.00.

Pieces of the Past; £6.90.

Guidecards:

Armagh Friary.

Ballycopeland Windmill.

Banagher & Bonevagh Churches.

Beaghmore Stone Circles.

Bonamargy Friary.

Carrickfergus Castle.

Devenish Monastic Site.

Dundrum.

Dungiven Priory & Bawn.

Dunluce Castle.

Enniskillen Castle.

Greencastle.

Greyabbey.

Hillsborough Fort.

Inch Abbey.

Jordan's Castle.

Monea Castle.

Navan Fort.

Nendrum.

St Patrick in Co Down.

Three Tower Houses.

Tully Castle.

White Island & Innishmacsaint.

Leaflets:

Caring for Historic Monuments.

Farming & the Historic Landscape.

Treasure Hunting, Archaeology & the Law.

Irish Archaeology – an Introductory Booklist.

Heritage of Northern Ireland.

Care of Graveyards.

Recognising Irish Antiquities.

Understanding Historic Monuments on the Farm.

Carrickfergus Castle Discovery Book.

Young Archaeologists Leaflet.

Postcards:

Ardboe Cross.

Audley's Castle.

Ballycopeland Windmill.

Ballymacdermott Cairn.

Bonamargy Friary.

Carrickfergus Castle.

Devenish Cross.

Dundrum Castle.

Dunluce Towers.

Dunluce Cliffs.

Giants Ring.

Goward Dolmen.

Greencastle.

Greyabbey.

Harry Avery's Castle.

Hillsborough Fort.

Inch Abbey.

Jordan's Castle.

Kilclief Castle.

Mound of Down.

Narrow Water Castle.

Navan Fort.

Nendrum Monastery.

Ossian's Grave.

Strangford Castle.

Struell Wells.

White Island Stone Figures.

Prints:

Great Wedding Feast, Hillsborough Castle.

Two full colour prints; £18.00 each, £32.00 per pair.

Slidepacks:

Early Irish Stone Carving; £1.25.

One Thousand Years of Defence; £2.50.

DERRY FILM & VIDEO

Geraldine McColgan, Derry Film and Video, 1 Westend Park, Derry BT48 9JF.
Tel: 0504 260128. Fax: 0504 260326.

Video:

Mother Ireland; VHS; £12.00 (inc p&p).

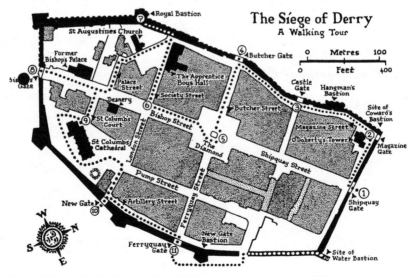

From *Blackened with hunger* (North-West Archaeological and Historical Society)

DOWN ARTS CENTRE

Rita Crawley, Down Arts Centre, 2–6 Irish Street, Downpatrick,
Co Down BT30 6BP.
Tel: 0396 615283.

The Centre aims to provide music, drama, visual arts, craft
events, workshops and classes for adults and children to explore
and question the cultural heritage of Ireland and other
countries. It offers an unusual range of resources and services for
hire.

EMU Workshops & Performances:

Armagh Rhymers; £150.00.
>An interactive show which presents a dramatic show of music,
>song, poetry and dance and encourages children to participate. An
>accompanying exhibition stimulates expression of opinion on what
>has been seen.

Victorian Music Hall Day; £125.00.
>Song. comedy and melodrama using group work, performance,
>improvisation, dressing-up and good fun.

Exhibitions:

Mother Ireland & Loyalist Ladies; available 5/92; £50.00 (plus onward
>travel).
>Photographic exhibition analysing the many kinds of female
>imagery used to symbolise Ireland and the small but powerful
>range of female emblems employed by the loyalist community in
>Northern Ireland.

Wallpaintings in Northern Ireland; available 3/92; £50.00 (plus onward
>travel).
>Designed to show the many living roles of wallpaintings with
>sections on history, unveilings, commemoration, territory, protest,
>fun and community, repainting and destruction. Carefully balance
>of loyalist and nationalist examples.

Slide Lectures (ages 14+):

Mother Ireland & Loyalist Ladies; £45.00 (plus expenses).
>A pictorial history of the various female figures emblamatic of
>Ireland, together with some of the main female symbols employed
>by the loyalist community.

Will the Real King Billy Please Stand Up?; £45.00 (plus expenses).
    The use and transformation of the image of William III in fine and
    popular art and living traditions.

Nationalist Imagery; £45.00 (plus expenses).
    Historical survey of the various stages by which such symbols as
    Celtic imagery, the harp, the shamrock, the colour green and the
    tricolour flag became absorbed and successively reinterpreted by
    the Irish nationalist tradition.

Orange Symbolism; £45.00 (plus expenses).
    An analytical history of the main symbols associated with
    Orangeism and loyalism including lilies, drums, sashes, banners,
    Biblical emblems, masonic imagery, swords, arches, bonfires,
    effigies and heraldry.

From *The siege of Derry 1689* (Guildhall Press)

DOWN COUNTY MUSEUM

Gerard Lennon, Down County Museum, The Mall, Downpatrick, Co Down.
Tel: 0396 615022/615218.

The Museum has been created to collect, conserve, interpret and display those objects which best serve to illustrate the history of County Down and to research related subjects. The study of human history is understood to include concern with the natural environment and with appropriate expressions of the arts and crafts, past and present.

Books:

Down Under: County Down Links With Australia; Richard Reid; 1990.

Walk About Downpatrick; D P McGrady & B S Turner; 1986.

Walk About Newcastle; Newcastle Field Club; 1986.

Walk About Saintfield; Enid Minnis; 1985.

Information sheets:

Geology of County Down; Philip Doughty; 1988.

Man from God-Knows-Where; 1990.

Saint Patrick; Brian S Turner; 1990.

Resources:

Images from County Down Museum.
  Sixteen A3 posters reflecting the major themes of the museum and the rich cultural heritage of County Down.

Colouring card series.
  Irish Woodkern, John de Courcy, Saint Patrick and Southwell Schoolboy.

Jigsaws.
  Down County Museum, Governor's Residence, John de Courcy, Saint Patrick.

Postcards.

ECLIPSE PROMOTIONS

Roger Wort, Gavin Smyth Booksellers, 245 Lisburn Road, Belfast BT9 7EN.
Tel: 0232 668033

Eclipse Promotions produce Folkcraft Films to foster and develop an interest in traditional Ulster community crafts, cultural activities and social customs through a continuing series of educational videos, aimed mainly at upper primary and lower secondary schools but also suitable for any type of cultural heritage and cross-community project.

Videos:

Bodhran Maker.

Open Hearth Baker.

Punch & Judy Man.

Straw Man.

Toy Maker.

Videos Forthcoming:

Blacksmith.

Half Door Dancer.

Shoemaker.

Tinsmith.

Willow Worker.

EDUCATION & LIBRARY BOARDS

The Editor, Northern Ireland Bibliography, North Eastern
Education & Library Board, Demesne Avenue, Ballymena, Co
Antrim BT43 7BG.
Tel: 0266 41531/2/3. Fax: 0266 46680.

The five public library services of Northern Ireland jointly
publish the Northern Ireland Bibliography for which
contributions are also received from the Linen Hall Library, the
Ulster Folk & Transport Museum, the Ulster Museum and the
Ulster-American Folk Park. Earlier issues were published under
the title of Northern Ireland Local Studies (1–17, 1981–86) and
Local Studies (18–26, 1987–90).

Publication:

Northern Ireland Bibliography; Library Service, North Eastern Education
& Library Board (ed); 1991.
Attempts to show the range of literature of Northern Ireland
interest currently being published. Selected government
publications, 'non-book' material, and interesting newspaper and
magazine articles are also included.

BELFAST ELB

Secondary Schools Library Service, Belfast Education & Library Board, Ulidia Centre for Resources & Training, Somerset Street, Belfast BT7 2GS.
Tel: 0232 491058.

The BELB is concerned with the provision of advisory and support service for schools which are developing opportunities for their pupils to learn about and appreciate their own cultural traditions, and the traditions of others, in an informed way.

Publications:

Fiction Booklists No 2: Novels Set in Northern Ireland for First to Third Forms; BELB Secondary Schools Library Service; 1990.

Teaching Pack:

Irish Presbyterians; 1989; [GCSE].
The Church in the modern world.

The Ligoniel Horse Bus, from *Belfast women* (NICEA Vol. 1)

NORTH EASTERN ELB

Lynn Buick, Reference Librarian – Local Studies, Library
Service, North Eastern Education & Library Board, Area Library
Headquarters, Demesne Avenue, Ballymena, Co Antrim
BT43 7BG.
Tel: 0266 41531. Fax: 0266 46680.

The Library Service aims to collect all published and 'semi-published' local studies material in all suitable formats, to encourage the production of such material and to produce its own, as appropriate. It provides access to such items, and sets them in the wider context of similar material relating to other cultures and societies, languages and literature.

Publication:

Local Studies Quarterly Additions List.

Resources:

Books and pamphlets.

Local history packs.
   Subject and topographical packs of photocopied material.

Maps.

Newspapers.

Photographs (mainly from the Lawrence Collection).

Reading lists.
   On specific topics or places.

SOUTH EASTERN ELB

Laura Plummer, Assistant Chief Librarian, Education & Young People, South Eastern Education & Library Board, Windmill Hill, Ballynahinch, Co Down BT24 8DH.
Tel: 0238 562639. Fax: 0238 565072.

The SEELB Library Service holdings include a wide range of books, maps, journals and newspapers as well as audio-visual materials relating to them; there is strong emphasis on County Down and south Antrim.. Staff in the Irish and Local Studies Section and the Education and Young People Department at Library Headquarters will answer queries, give talks and mount displays on request.

Educational Materials:

Sennachies.
   Children's fiction by Irish authors.

Folk & Fairy Tales of Ireland for Key Stages I & II.

Irish Fiction for Key Stage III.

Irish Music.

Irish Names for Key Stage III.

Irish Poetry for Key Stage IV.

Myths and Legends for Key Stage I.

Myths and Legends for Key Stage II.

Local History Resources:

Irish and local studies leaflet.

Local history packs.

Local history source lists.

Maps.

Northern Ireland bibliography.

Photographs.

Postcards.

Teacher's guide to local history collection.

Videos.

Newspaper Indices:

Index to the County Down Spectator, 1904–64; Jack McCoy; 1983; £1.50.

Index to the Downpatrick Recorder, 1836–86; Jack McCoy; 1987; £5.00.

Index to the Mourne Observer, 1949–80; Jack McCoy; 1984; £2.00.

Index to the Newtownards Chronicle, 1873–1900, & the Newtownards Independent, 1871–73; Kenneth Robinson; 1990; £3.00.

Teaching Aids:

Local History Packs; Helen Barnes; 1990; free.

Local History Projects: What the Teacher Needs to Know; 2nd ed, 1986; free.

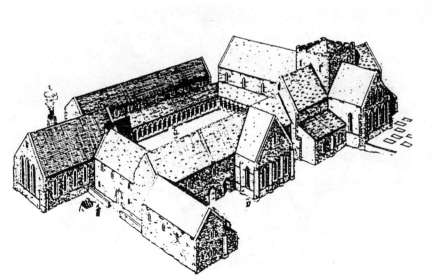

Reconstruction of Grey Abbey monastery, Co. Down (Crown copyright)

SOUTHERN ELB

Library Service, Southern Education & Library Board, Library Headquarters, 1 Markethill Road, Armagh BT60 1NR. Tel: 0861 525353. Fax: 0861 526879.

The SELB endeavours tomaintain an Irish collection which is wide-ranging in both scope and format. It seeks to provide information on all aspects of Irish life, past and present, utilising not just books and micro-film but videos, audio cassettes, compact discs, maps, postcards and photographs as well. The Library Service has compiled a number of media lists relevant to cultural heritage and is always willing to consider publishing lists of books and audio-visual materials on request.

Estyn Evans drawing of Mourne wall (*Varieties of Irishness* IIS)

WESTERN ELB

Library Service, Western Education & Library Board, Divisional Headquarters, Hospital Road, Omagh, Co Tyrone.
Tel: 0662 240240.

The WELB aims to provide information on all aspects of history, life and traditions in Ireland to all sections of the community. Items listed are available from the Irish and Local Studies Departments of Enniskillen and Omagh libraries.

Book:

Images of Fermanagh: Reminiscence & Recall; G McKinley & K Palmer; 1989.

Catalogues:

Books of Irish Interest.
    Twice yearly list of additions to stock of the Irish and Local Studies Department in the Tyrone Division of the Library Service.

Local History Sources: Fermanagh Division; F J Nawn & Kate McAllister; 1982.

Local History Sources: Tyrone Division; Kate McAllister; 1982.

From *Images of Stone* (Fermanagh County Museum)

EDUCATIONAL COMPANY

Educational Company Ltd, 1 Mallusk Park, Mallusk Road, Newtownabbey, Co Antrim BT36 8GW.

The Educational Company is concerned with the application of cultural heritage to the Northern Ireland schools curriculum.

Forthcoming Book:

Ulster Images: Cultural Heritage Miscellany.

Ballykeel dolmen, from *Mullaghbawn Folklore and Historical Society* (Vol. 4)

EUROPEAN STUDIES PROJECT

Bob McKinley, Field Officer Northern Ireland, European Studies Project, Ulster Folk & Transport Museum, Cultra Manor, 153 Bangor Road, Cultra, Co Down BT18 0EU.
Tel: 023 17 5285. Fax: 023 17 7992.

The European Studies Project is a six year curriculum development programme, funded for the period 1986–92. It runs one scheme each for the 11–14 and 14–16 age groups and two for students of 16–18. Together these programmes currently involve ninety schools, 400 teachers and 11,000 students and they are co-ordinated by a full-time Director and five Field Officers. The project's philosophy is predicated on the fact of 'Europe' including the islands of Great Britain and Ireland and it's steering committee includes representatives of the Departments of Education in Northern Ireland, England and the Republic of Ireland and of the European Commission.

Study Units:

Unit 1;   The Normans: Case Studies in Ireland, Britain & Europe.

Unit 2;   Water: a Precious Resource.

Unit 3;   Plantation, Our Shared Experience: Colonization in the 17th Century.

Unit 4;   Attitudes to Conflict: Ireland, Britain & Europe, 1914–21.

Unit 5;   Migration.

FEDERATION FOR ULSTER LOCAL STUDIES

The Development Officer, Federation for Ulster Local Studies, Institute of Irish Studies, 8 Fitzwilliam Street, Belfast BT9 6AW. Tel/Fax: 0232 235254.

The Federation works with local history societies; represents the interests of the local historian to the government and the public; encourages local research and publications; provides information sheets on local history, fund raising, historic monuments etc; produces newsletters on what is happening amongst societies; publishes its own journal full of articles, reviews and information; and has public liability insurance cover for its members.

Book:

Every Stoney Acre Has a Name: a Celebration of the Townland in Ulster; Tony Canavan (ed); 1991; £3.50.

Journal:

Ulster Local Studies; twice yearly.

Newsletter:

Local History Link; Doreen Corcoran (ed); February & September..

Resources:

Contact names and addresses for local history societies.

Information sheets on townlands and historic buildings and monuments.

Services:

Seminars, workshops and conferences.

Reference service for speakers on local history.

Guidelines on research.

FERMANAGH COUNTY MUSEUM

Fermanagh County Museum, Castle Barracks, Enniskillen, Co
Fermanagh BT74 7HL.
Tel: 0365 325050.

The Museum is concerned with cultural traditions relating to
County Fermanagh and covering such fields as crafts, music and
oral history.

Books:

Forthill Park; Recreation Department; £0.50.
> Detailed descriptions of the park's trees and its seventeenth
> century earthen fort.

Images of Stone: Figure Sculpture of the Lough Erne Basin; Helen Hickey;
£3.95.
> Figure sculpture in the Lough Erne basin over the last two
> millenia, ranging from the famous prehistoric idols of Boa Island
> to the more recent folk-art carvings of Derrylin. This new edition
> includes a location map and index.

Teaching/Information Packs:

History On Your Doorstep: Monastic Settlement; 1989; [S].
> A collection of written and pictorial source material relating to the
> early Christian monastery on Devenish Island in Lower Lough
> Erne. Ideal for training students in interpretation of historical
> evidence with its frequent ambiguities and discrepancies.

History On Your Doorstep: Rural Life in Fermanagh; Helen Lanigan Wood;
1989.
> Illustrated booklet covering many aspects of country life in bygone
> days: agriculture, care of livestock, poteen making, seasonal
> customs and the crafts of scythe-stone making and rush and straw
> work.

Traditional Music in Schools; 1990; [ages 8–16].
> Teachers' pack including booklet and tapes.

Videos:

Devenish Island: Monastic Settlement; 1985; £10.80; [S].
> The history of Devenish Island since the founding of its monastery
> by Saint Molaise in the sixth century. Ideal preparation for school
> visits.

Maguires of Fermanagh & the Town of Enniskillen; 1985; £25.00.
    A description of life in medieval Fermanagh under the rule of the
    Maguires, the troubled times of the Elizabethan wars, the
    Plantation, the emergence of new towns and the achievements of
    the prosperous eighteenth century.

Forthcoming:

Teaching & Information Packs: Fermanagh Folk series, *From Cottages to
    Castles & Food in Fermanagh*; 1992; [ages 8–13].

Video: *Enniskillen Today & Yesterday*; 1993.

From *History on your doorstep: rural life in Fermanagh* (Fermanagh County
Museum)

FLYING FOX FILMS

Flying Fox Films, 37 Queen Street, Belfast BT1 6EA.
Tel: 0232 244811/245301. Fax: 0232 2324699.

Flying Fox is an independent production company specializing in films about literature, the arts and the folklife of Ireland.

Book:

Steelchest, Nail in the Boot & the Barking Dog; David Hammond; 1986.
    Folklore.

Films:

Frank Orr: Lambeg Drummer; David Hammond; 1988.
    Folklore.

Hidden Ground: Thomas Flanagan; David Hammond; 1988.

Hidden Pursuits; James Skelly; 1991.
    Local history.

Magic Fiddle; David Hammond; 1991.
    Folklore.

Mountain, Fen & Lake; David Hammond; 1991.

Space For Dreaming; David Hammond; 1989.
    Biography: E Estyn Evans.

Steelchest, Nail in the Boot & the Barking Dog; David Hammond; 1986.
    Folklore.

Where Your Face Is Known; James Skelly; 1991.
    History of settlement.

From *Sing a song and play it*(Armagh Pipers' Club)

FORTNIGHT EDUCATIONAL TRUST

Chris Moffat, Fortnight Educational Trust, 7 Lower Crescent, Belfast BT7 1NR.
Tel: 0232 236575. Fax: 0232 232650.

The FET has been set up to promote education and understanding through the stimulation of debate on social, political, economic and cultural issues. Funded by the Joseph Rowntree Charitable Trust and the Northern Ireland Voluntary Trust, FET itself has charitable status. Its work focuses on publications (particularly supplements to 'Fortnight' magazine) and public debate (seminars and conferences).

Book:

Cattle Rustling: an Illuminated Script to be Told, Read or Played; James Simmons and Mervyn Turner; £4.50.
A powerful and dramatic illustrated retelling of the Tain in prose and verse, in the form of a two act play. Prepared specifically with teachers and pupils in mind, it includes production ideas, notes and further references.

Resource:

Booklet of draft/trial curriculum materials on the background to the hero legends
Referenced to KS3 and 4, Cultural Heritage and EMU cross-curricular educational themes and elements of programmes of study in English, Drama, History, RE and Art & Design (AL 4–10).

Supplements to 'Fortnight' Magazine:

Free Thought in Ireland.
Dissenters and dissenting traditions.

Literary Supplements:
Samuel Beckett;
John Hewitt;
Stuart Parker;
W B Yeats.

Opening the Field.
Rural Perspectives.

Radical Ulster.
Joseph Tomelty, Peader O'Donnell & Sam Hanna Bell.

Religion in Ireland.

Sexual Subjects.
    Women and sexuality in Ireland.

Varieties of Irishness.
    Abridged lecture to first Cultural Traditions Conference by Roy
    Foster.

Voyages of Discovery.
    Emigration.

Forthcoming:

Literary Supplements to 'Fortnight':
    Michael MacLaverty;
    Janet McNeil;
    Forrest Reid.

On board the brig 'Union', from *Across the Atlantic* (Ulster American Folk Park)

FRIAR'S BUSH PRESS

Friar's Bush Press, 24 College Park Avenue, Belfast BT7 1LR. Tel: 0232 327695.

Friar's Bush is a publisher of books of historic interest with an emphasis on the use of historical photographs to reveal social, economic and architectural traditions; the use of firsthand accounts to reveal social history; and the reprinting of historical primary and secondary source material.

Books:

1789: a Belfast Chronicle; James McAllister; £12.50.
   A unique record of life 200 years ago, from the original files of 'The Newsletter'.

Armagh; Roger Weatherup; £4.95.
   Historic photographs of the primatial city.

Band Played On; Gerald Rafferty; £4.95.
   Humorous stories of rural life by a popular local journalist.

Caught in Time; W A Maguire; £7.50.
   The photographs of Alex Hogg of Belfast, 1870–1939.

Enniskillen: Historical Images of an Island Town; Helen Lanigan Wood; £4.95.
   The story of the town told through photographs, including architecture and social and economic activities.

Farming in Ulster; Jonathon Bell and Mervyn Watson; £4.50.
   A unique collection of historic photographs.

Fermanagh Childhood; William K Parke; £4.50.
   Village life in Ulster, fifty years ago.

From the Mountains to the Sea; Ben Corr; £4.95.
   Photographs of the people of Mourne, 1955–75.

Heydays, Fair-Days & Not-So-Good Old Days; W A Maguire; £3.50.
   A volume of family photographs taken about eighty years ago by Charles Langham of Tempo Manor. It conveys a vivid picture of life in the village and manor of Tempo when the latter was in its heyday and the monthly fair an important occasion.

In Belfast Town: Early Photographs from the Lawrence Collection, 1864–80; Brian M Walker and Hugh Dixon; £4.95.
   Earliest collection of photographs of Victorian Belfast.

In Sunshine or in Shadow; D Bigger and T MacDonald; £7.50.
A major collection of photographs from 'The Derry Standard', 1928–39.

James Boyce is Late; Jack Claypole; £4.95.
Tale of a village school and country life.

Journey through Lecale: Historic Photographs from the W A Green Collection at the Ulster Folk & Transport Museum, 1910–39; John Magee; £7.50.
Photographs of the Kingdom of Lecale during the early decades of the twentieth century; a rich variety of sea and land, town and village, with informed commentary by Jack Magee.

Looking Back; Arthur Campbell; £4.95.
An evocative book featuring scenes from Dublin and Belfast, 1939–60.

Newry, Warrenpoint & Rostrevor; Fergus Hanna Bell; £4.95.
Photographs from the Lawrence Collection, 1865–80.

On the Banks of the Foyle; Brian Mitchell; £4.95.
Historic photographs of Victorian and Edwardian Derry.

Post 381: the Memoirs of a Belfast Air Raid Warden; James Doherty; £4.95.
Railways in Ulster; Grenfell Morton; £4.95.

Road to the Glens; Cahal Dallat; £4.95.
Historic photographs of the Antrim coast and the Glens.

Sailing the Seaways: Historic Maritime Photographs from the Ulster Folk & Transport Museum, 1864–1920; Michael McCaughan; £4.95.
Photographs of working boats with echoes of a bygone age of tall ships.

Sentry Hill: an Ulster Farm & Family; Brian M Walker; £7.50.
Revised edition of the very successful study of a farm and family through diaries, letters and photographs.

Ships & Quaysides of Ulster; Robert Anderson and Ian Wilson; £4.95.

Steel Ships & Iron Men; Michael McCaughan; £4.95.
Historic photographs from the shipbuilders Harland & Wolff.

Tour of East Antrim; Doreen Corcoran; £4.95.
Historic photographs from Larne to Carrick, via Whitehead and Islandmagee.

Tour of North Down; Jane E M Crosbie; £4.95.
Historic photographs of the coastal towns.

Tour of the Ardes; Jane E M Crosbie; £4.95.
Historic photographs of the Ards peninsula and north-east Down.

Tour of the Causeway Coast; Cahal Dallat; £4.95.
  Historic photographs of the towns and villages of north Antrim and the Giant's Causeway.

Tour of the Mournes: Historic Photographs from the W A Green Collection at the Ulster Folk & Transport Museum, 1910–39; Fred Hamond and Tom Porter; £4.95.
  Delightful views of Newcastle, Kilkeel and Annalong; coastal roads and mountain peaks as seen by visitors in the first decades of the century.

Under the Big Lamp; Sheela Speers; £4.95.
  Historic photographs of Carrickfergus.

Victorian & Edwardian Newcastle; Grenfell Morton; £4.50.
  A comprehensively illustrated history.

Where the Six Mile Water Flows; Jack McKinney; £4.95.
  Historic photographs of Ballyclare.

THE CORPORATION BELLMAN OF BELFAST.

From *1789: a Belfast Chronicle* (Friars Bush Press)

GAEL-LINN

Gael-Linn, 62a Upper English Street, Armagh BT61 7LG.
Tel/Fax: 0861 522162.

Gael-Linn is a non-political and non-sectarian educational and cultural organisation whose central aim is to promote a wider appreciation of the Irish language and cultural heritage throughout Ireland.

Publication:

An Dreimire.
> A special Irish language publication for A-level students and containing relevant poetry, essay and prose material in a newspaper format.

Resources:

Traditional music and song on record, cassette and compact disc.

Information Leaflets:

Extra-curricular Irish language activities.
> For school students of various levels and abilities, including a table quiz, essay and debating competitions.

Slógadh.
> A youth festival with a wide range of arts related to educational activities.

Traditional music and song.
> Indicates the use of particular recordings to illustrate traditional instruments and various types and styles of music and song, as well as their influence on some contemporary and popular groups.

Services:

Irish summer courses in the Donegal Gaeltacht and special scholarship scheme.

Video:

Mise Eire.
> Feature length film made in 1959, using original newsreel footage to illustrate events in Ireland in the early years of this century. narration is in Irish but comprehensive notes in English are included.

Forthcoming:

Irish Language Pedagogic Package, in co-operation with the Northern
    Ireland Association of Teachers of Irish; 1992/3.
    Linguistic material aligned to living Irish songs to engage young
    people's attention to Irish as a foreign language. Three music
    cassettes aimed at different age groups (4–8, 9–13 and 13+) plus
    worksheets for learners and teachers' notes.

From *The Tale of Deirdre* (Navan Research Group)

GLENS OF ANTRIM HISTORICAL SOCIETY

Dr Cahal Dallat, Glens of Antrim Historical Society, 'Drimargy', 9 Atlantic Avenue, Ballycastle, Co Antrim BT54 6AL.

The Society aims to study the history, traditions and folklore of the Glens of Antrim and to preserve historical knowledge and objects of historical interest.

Books:

Maybe It Was Yesterday; Cahal Dallat et al; 1976; [ages 12–18].
  History through old photographs.

Andrew Nicholl's Paintings of the Antrim Coast; Cahal Dallat & Jimmy Irvine (eds); 1982; [ages 16–19].
  Collection of paintings completed in 1828, with notes. good examples of life in the early nineteenth century.

Day of the Corncrake; John Hewitt & Charles McAuley; 1984; [ages 12–19].
  Heritage of the Glens in poetry and pictures.

McCahan's Local Histories; Cahal Dallat (ed); 1984; [ages 12–19].
  Cameos of places in north Antrim and the Glens: ideal for project work.

Journal:

Glynns: the Journal of the Glens of Antrim Historical Society; annual, 1973–present.
  Heritage articles including local history, place-names, surnames, customs etc.

GUILDHALL PRESS

Guildhall Press, 41 Great James Street, Derry BT48 7DF. Tel: 0504 264413.

Guildhall is a non-profit educational publisher whose general aim is to encourage and nurture an interest in local history and folklore. Time and resources are devoted to researching and recording the many facets of life from all sections of the community in the north-west of Ireland.

Books:

Across the Foyle; Anne Murray-Cavanagh; 1979.

Best of Jed; Sinead Coyle; 1990.

Derry Jail; Colm M Cavanagh; 1990.

Derry Quiz Book 2; 1988.

Derry's Shirt Tale; Geraldine McCarter; 1988.

Derry's Walls; Paul Hippsley; 1991.

Folly Up; Seamus McConnell; 1990.

George Farquhar; Kathleen Carlin; 1989.

Hiring Fairs in Derry, Tyrone & Donegal; George Sweeney; 1989.

Just For a Laugh; 1988; [ages 8–11].
      Jokes.

O'Doherty Historic Trail in Counties Derry & Donegal; Murray Dougherty; 1989.

Parade of Phantoms; Peter McCartney; 1991.

Siege of Derry, 1689; Peter McCartney; 1988.

Talk of the Town; Seamus McConnell; 1989.
      Derry colloquialism.

There Was Music There in the Derry Air; 1989.

What About the Workers; 1989.

Wordsmiths; 1990.

George Walker, Governor of Londonderry; George Sweeney; 1989.

Forthcoming:

Churches; 2/92.
> History of all the churches in the Derry area.

Derry Doodles; 11/91.
> Puzzle book.

Hiring Fairs & Farm Workers in the North-West of Ireland; 3/92.

Springtown Chronicles; 12/91.
> Story of the American military camp at Springtown.

Then & Now; 6/92.
> Photographic record of Derry through the decades.

From *The siege of Derry 1689* (Guildhall Press)

INSTITUTE OF IRISH STUDIES

The Institute of Irish Studies, The Queen's University of Belfast, Belfast BT7 1NN.
Tel: 0232 245133.

The Institute was established in 1965 to facilitate research in all disciplines related to Ireland. Current activities cover a wide spectrum: history, archaeology, architecture, anthropology, politics, language and literature. The Institute's publishing policy aims to reflect the breadth and nature of such interests.

Books:

Archaeology of Ireland: from Colonisation to Plantation; J P Mallory & T E McNeill; £15.00/£7.50.
An insight into the current debate on the importance of different explain the development of Ulster society and landscape from its initial colonisation by hunting bands in Neolithic times to the Plantation of the more modern period.

Aspects of Irish Studies; Myrtle Hill & Sarah Barber (eds); £4.95.
Includes papers by historians, linguists, political scientists and social anthropologists.

Contributions to a Comparative Study of Ulster, Irish & Scottish Gaelic; Colm O'Báoill; £7.50.

Cultural Traditions in Northern Ireland; Maurna Crozier (ed).
An insight into the current debate on the importance of different cultural traditions in the community:
Vol 1 – 'Varieties of Irishness'; £2.95.
Vol 2 – 'Varieties of Britishness'; £3.95.
Vol 3 – 'All Europeans Now?'; £3.95.

Culture in Ireland: Division or Diversity?; Edna Longley (ed); £4.25.
Proceedings of a conference organised by the Cultures of Ireland Group, including papers by President Mary Robinson, Jennifer Johnston and Brendan Kenelly.

Culture, Identity and Broadcasting in Ireland: Local Issues, Global Perspectives; Martin McLoone (ed); £4.50.
Proceedings of the Cultural Traditions Group/Media Studies, UUC Symposium.

Dialects of Ulster Irish; Cathair O'Dochartaigh; £7.50.
First modern broad scaled discussion of internal differentiation within Ulster Irish dialects.

53

Freedom from Fear: Churches Together in Northern Ireland; Simon
Lee (ed); £3.50.
Reports on the churches' contributions to reconciliation through
community work.

Parishes of Ulster – Vols 1–38; £15.00/£7.50.
Ordnance Survey Memoirs offering unique material on life at
parish level 150 years ago.

Printed Word & the Common Man: Popular Culture in Ulster, 1700–1900; J
R R Adams; £12.50.
Unearths for the first time the vast range of printed material used
by ordinary people in the eighteenth and nineteenth centuries.

Royal Irish Constabulary: an Oral History; John D Brewer; £6.50.
Provides a unique history of the RIC in the years shortly before its
disbandment in 1922.

Strangford Lough: the Wildlife of an Irish Sea Lough; Robert Brown;
£15.00/£9.50.
This unique study will appeal to all interested in wildlife as well as
those with a special interest in the loch.

Ulster Politics: the Formative Years, 1868–86; B M Walker; £15.00.
An important study of the changes in politics and society in Ulster,
illustrating the developments of the period which resulted in the
rise of present day issues. Published with the Ulster Historical
Foundation.

Journal:

Irish Review, twice annually.
Interdisciplinary journal for cultural, historical and literary studies.

Forthcoming:

Dictionary of Northern Ireland Biographies; Kate Newmann; 6/92.

Parliamentary Election Results in Ireland, 1918–91; B M Walker; 6/92.
Includes Dáil Éireann results, elections to Westminster and
Northern Ireland parliaments and assemblies.

Traditional Music: Whose Music? Cultural Traditions in Ireland; Peter
McNamee (ed); 2/92.
Proceedings of a 1991 Co-Operation North conference which discussed
the role and 'ownership' of traditional music.

Vision & Reality: a Survey of Irish Inter-Church Relations, 1904–91; Ian Ellis;
6/92.

Who Cared? Charity in Victorian Belfast; Alison Jordan; 6/92.

Examines a hitherto neglected aspect of social history, looking at the many charitable bodies in nineteenth century Belfast.

From *Who cared: charity in Victorian Belfast* (IIS)

IRISH WORLD

Irish World, Irish World House, 26 Market Square, Dungannon, Co Tyrone BT70 1AB.
Tel: 086 87 24187.

Irish World researches and publishes material within the ambit of local studies – principally encompassing themes such as history, genealogy, folklore, dialect and archaeology – that is adjudged to be of educational or cultural value and which is likely to appeal across a wide range of interests and viewpoints.

Books:

You Don't Say; William O'Kane (ed); 1991.
   Dialect dictionary.

Carrickmore Tradition; Eoin Kerr; 1984.
   Sport history.

Cursing Stone; Peter Makem; 1990.
   Poetry and mythology.

Journal:

Linnet; William O'Kane and Maggie Reilly (eds); occasional..

Video:

Ireland's World; Don Farrell; 1988.
   History and emigration.

Forthcoming Book:

Townlands & Parishes of Co Tyrone; Eoin Kerr et al; summer/92.
   History of land division.

ISLAND PUBLICATIONS

Michael Hall, 132 Serpentine Road, Newtownabbey, Co Antrim BT36 7JQ.
Tel: 0232 778771.

Island Publications is an independent publisher of material of Irish interest, particularly relating to the heroic period.

Books:

Cúchulainn, Champion of Ulster; Michael Hall; £3.90.

Twenty Years: a Concise Chronology of Events in Northern Ireland, 1968–88; £4.95.

Resources:

Cúchulainn; poster; £1.50.

Historic Ulster; 24' x 17' map; £2.70 (rolled), £18.50 (block-mounted).

Services:

Kinder Community House.
> Residential centre for thirty people, located in Killough, Co Down. Equipped with maps and informative posters for heritage explorations.

LINEN HALL LIBRARY

Linen Hall Library, 17 Donegall Square North, Belfast BT1 5GD. Tel: 0232 321707.

Linen Hall is a subscription library which holds collections of manuscripts, books and other documents for consultation and loan – including Irish and local history, Northern Ireland politics (with over 50,000 items), and genealogy (including many individual family histories) – and publishes printed items and a wide range of local illustrative material, particularly 16th–19th century maps, William Conor and Tom Carr reproductions, and original prints by Jean Duncan, David Evans and Raymond Piper.

Publications:

Belfast Scenery in Thirty Views; E K Proctor; £12.25.
  Reprint of original 1832 edition.

History of the Linen Hall Library; John Killen; £15.00.

LISBURN MUSEUM

Lisburn Museum, The Assembly Rooms, Market Square, Lisburn, Co Antrim.
Tel: 0846 672624.

The Museum collects and interprets artefacts and information relating to south-west Antrim and the Lagan Valley.

Collections on Display:

Lagan Valley Linen Industry.

Lagan Valley Transport.

Lisburn, 1912–22, the Ulster Crisis & the Great War.

On the Home Front, Lisburn 1939–45.

Book:

Hugenots & Ulster, 1685–1985; W A Maguire et al; 1985; £3.50.

Information Sheets:

Market House, Assembly Rooms, Museum; 1985; £0.10.

Moira, an Outline History; 1987; £0.10.

Resources:

Irish linen industry reference library.

Lisburn and Lagan Valley local studies reference library.

Old photographs of Lisburn and the Lagan Valley.

Historic maps of the area.

Video Reference Library:

Battle of the Somme; Imperial War Museum.

Linen industry (various).

Local history (various).

Traditional crafts.
    Linked with textiles, lace-making and patchwork collections and
    displays.

MOYLE DISTRICT COUNCIL

Moyle District Council, Sheskburn House, 7 Mary Street,
Ballycastle, Co Antrim BT54 6QH.
Tel (Giant's Causeway Visitors' Centre): 026 57 31855.

Northern Ireland's smallest district council area includes one of
its most enduring tourist attractions, the Giant's Causeway. As
well as being the appropriate starting point for visits, the
Causeway Visitor's Centre holds resources useful for cultural
traditions studies.

Videos:

Day for Being Irish; David & Joy Barrow; 1986.
    Lammas Fair.

Song of Ulster; Robert Blair & Tony McAuley; 1986.

MULLAGHBAWN FOLKLORE & HISTORICAL SOCIETY

Mullaghbawn Folklore & Historical Society, Mullaghbawn Folk Museum, Tullymacrieve, Mullaghbawn, Newry, Co Down. Tel (Secretary: Mrs Nora McCoy): 0693 888278.

The Society records the history, folklore, music, crafts and folk traditions of the past and works to sustain those still surviving in the area. Its focus is a folk museum, a two roomed cottage furnished in the style of the latter part of the nineteenth century.

Books:

Flaxmills; Una Walsh; 1988.

Gravestone Inscriptions in Mullaghbawn Churchyard; Una Walsh; 1989; [PS].

Journal:

Mullaghbawn Folklore & Historical Society; Patricia Mackey (ed); Vols I–IV, 1972–90.

Teaching Aids:

On site questionnaires; one copy available for duplication prior to visit: Around the fire, Buttermaking, Cottage crafts, Farm implements, General trail and Ironing in the 'Olden Days'.

Video:

Open Air Ceili; Michael McCoy; 1990. Available from Michael McCoy, c/o SAFE, Main Street, Camlough, Newry, Co Down.

Forthcoming:

Questionnaires: Candle making and Lamps.

Mullaghbawn Folklore & Historical Society; Vol V, 6/92.

NATIONAL TRUST

The National Trust, Northern Ireland Region, Rowallane House, Saintfield, Ballynahinch, Co Down BT24 7LH.
Tel: 0238 510721. Fax: 0238 511242.

As an independent charity, the Trust cares for eight historical houses, a flax beetling mill and a printing press in Northern Ireland, as well as large areas of unspoilt countryside and coastline. Support and assistance are provided to schools wishing to visit the properties to study the wide range of subjects associated with them.

Resources:

National Trust Education Supplement.

Northern Ireland 1992 Visitors Guide.
   Full details of all National Trust properties in Northern Ireland, including opening times and details of admission prices for school visits.

Young National Trust; (magazine).
   Education leaflets from Florence Court, Wellbrook, Springhill and Ardress, with details of arrangements for school visits and facilities.

Family handbook.

Guide books for major properties.

Information for visitors with disabilities.

National Trust handbooks.

Property leaflets.

Regional newsletters.

Strangford Lough brochure.
   Full colour brochure giving full details on wildlife and educational and interpretation facilities.

Teachers' Pack:

Springhill; Patricia Law; 1989.

Forthcoming Teachers' Pack:

Castleward; 1992.

NAVAN RESEARCH GROUP

Emania c/o Department of Archaeology, The Queen's
University of Belfast, Belfast BT7 1NN.

Navan Research Group undertakes and supports research on
Emain Macha, the ancient capital of Ulster, and through its
journal publishes articles on its archaeology, literature, history
and mythology, especially as they pertain to the Irish Iron Age
and the Ulster Cycle of tales.

Journal:

Emania: Bulletin of the Navan Research Group.

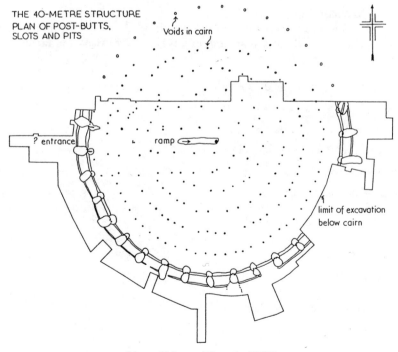

THE 40-METRE STRUCTURE
PLAN OF POST-BUTTS,
SLOTS AND PITS

Voids in cairn

? entrance

ramp

limit of excavation
below cairn

Plan of Navan (*Emania,* 1991)

NORTH DOWN HERITAGE CENTRE

North Down Heritage Centre, The Town Hall, Bangor,
Co Down BT20 4BT.
Tel: 0247 270371.

The Heritage Centre exists to reflect North Down's natural,
archaeological, historical and cultural heritage.

Books:

North Down Coastal Path; Ian Wilson (ed); 1986.

Ulster's Joan of Arc; Jack McCoy; 1989.
  The 1798 rebellion.

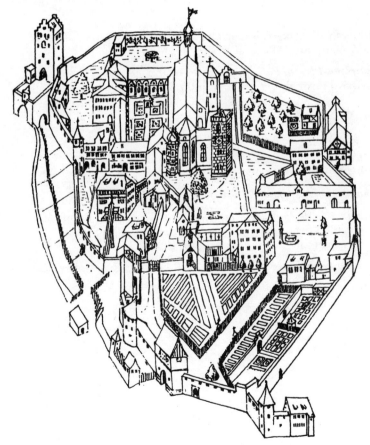

Precinct of the Abbey of St Gall, Switzerland, c.1660. The abbey was founded
in 612 by St Gall from Bangor (From *All European now?* IIS)

NORTH-WEST ARCHAEOLOGICAL &
HISTORICAL SOCIETY

K M Gormley, North-West Archaeological Society, 47 Aberfoyle Crescent, Londonderry BT48 7PG.
Tel: 0504 263854.

The Society brings together people from different cultural traditions to discuss, research and record their common heritage for the benefit of the community at large. This has resulted in the organisation of a number of lectures and exhibitions, as well as the publication of books and information packs.

Books:

Blackened with Hunger; K Gormley et al; 1989.
  Walking tour of the siege sites of Derry .

Picturesque, Planted Place; K Gormley et al; 1991.
  Drive through O'Cahan country.

Journal:

Templemore; Vols 1–3, 1985, 87 & 90.

Forthcoming Books:

Archaeology of Inishowen; M R Colhoun; 1992.

Placenames in the Parishes of Templemore & Clondermot; Pupils of St Cecilia's Secondary School, Clondermot High School & Templemore Secondary School; 1992.

Recording Gravestones of Lough Enagh; R Doherty & A Malley; 1992.

NORTHERN IRELAND CENTRE FOR LEARNING RESOURCES

Northern Ireland Centre for Learning Resources, The Orchard Building, Stranmillis College, Belfast BT9 5DY.
Tel: 0232 664525. Fax: 0232 681579.

The Centre designs and produces high level resources for education and training in Northern Ireland. Active in promoting the wider use of open learning and self-instructional media, NICLR produces interactive video disc resources, multi-media training packs, and a wide range of classroom resources designed for new curriculum needs.

Audio Tape Packs:

What's Time to a Pig?
Short stories from BBC Northern Ireland schools' radio programmes.

Today & Yesterday; Sam McBratney (ed).
Short stories from the BBC radio series of the same name.

Publications:

Investigating Place Names in Ulster; Jonathan Bardon.
A teachers' guide which includes sections on Gaelic, Viking, Anglo-Norman and English place names in Ulster. It provides historical background and explains many place names throughout the province.

Living & Working in Pre-Famine Ulster; John Dooher (ed).
A documentary selection of contemporary accounts of the 1830s, from the Ordnance Survey Memoirs.

Resource Packs:

Forest through the Year.
Focuses on local forests.

Home Rule: Personalities, Parties & Perceptions; Vivien Kelly & Stephen Cooke.
Introduces Key Stage 3 pupils to the issues at the heart of the debate centering on the Home Rule crisis of 1912–14. Accompanying computer material for the Apple Macintosh requires Hypercard 2.0 or later.

Just a Minute.
> Materials supporting work in English, History and Art & Design at all key stages, based on paintings and drawings of William Conor. Includes extension activities for other subjects.

Lagan Pack.
> From source to sea, the Lagan Canal and the linen industry.

Life in Ulster between the World Wars.

Living & Working in Pre-Famine Ulster.
> Contemporary accounts from the Ordnance Survey Memoirs of the 1930s.

Plantations.
> Teacher produced materials using a skills and evidence based approach to aid understanding of one of the historical foundations of division in Ireland.

Ulster & the World Wars.

Video Packs:

Castlecourt.
> Worksheets, slides, photographs and video for use in post-primary schools.

Farming.
> Farms and farm equipment of today and yesterday.

From Conflict to Co-Operation.
> Includes a video for post-primary schools on the events of the 1690s.

Joint Work in the Environment.
> Poster and video resulting from the Joint Work in the Environment Project which focused on combining fieldwork with use of IT. By compiling a database from local workhouse records, pupils uncovered evidence challenging traditional beliefs and enhancing understanding of a common inheritance.

Ulster-American Folk Park.
> Pupil and teacher videos to be used in conjunction with visits to the park.

NORTHERN IRELAND COMMUNITY EDUCATION ASSOCIATION

Northern Ireland Community Education Association, 25a University Road, Belfast BT7 1NA.
Tel: 0232 242717.

The Northern Ireland Community Education Association is an oral history and cross-community project encompassing Donegall Pass, the Markets and the lower Ormeau Road.

Booklets:

Belfast Women; 1991.

Blitz, the Soapworks and the Pam Pam; 1991.

Cures, Linen, Laundries; 1991.

Divvies, Coke & Black Soap; 1991.

Mary's Memories; 1991.

Forthcoming:

New booklets, an education pack with cross-curricular themes and a full 'professional' publication are planned for 1992.

NORTHERN IRELAND CURRICULUM COUNCIL

The Northern Ireland Curriculum Council, Stranmillis College, Stranmillis Road, Belfast BT9 5DY.
Tel: 0232 381271.

The Council was established to advise the Department of Education for Northern Ireland about what is taught in schools. It's central aim is to ensure that all pupils experience education that meets their needs and helps them to realise their full potential. Cultural Heritage is one of the six compulsory Educational Themes of the Education Reform Order (NI) 1989.

Publications:

Cross-Curricular Themes: Consultation Report; 1989.

Cross-Curricular Themes: Guidance Materials; 1990.

History: Consultation Report; 1991.

History: Guidance Materials; 1991.

NICC: a Guide; 1991.

NICC Update: Information Leaflet No 2; 1989.

Northern Ireland Curriculum: a Guide for Teachers; 1990.

NORTHERN IRELAND ENVIRONMENT LINK

Northern Ireland Environment Link, Armagh House, Ormeau
Avenue, Belfast BT2 8HB.
Tel: 0232 234393.

NIEL's main aim is to advance the education of the community
in environmental and ecological sciences by providing
information and facilities. It achieves this by acting as a linking
organisation for voluntary groups in Northern Ireland who are
concerned with the environment and conservation of the
countryside and wildlife.

Book:

Our Countryside: Our Concern; Kay Milton; 1990.

Typical Ulster gateposts by Raymond Piper from *Varieties of Britishness* (IIS)

NORTHERN IRELAND HERITAGE GARDENS COMMITTEE

Northern Ireland Heritage Gardens Committee, c/o Ulster Architectural Heritage Society, 181a Stranmillis Road, Belfast BT9 5DU.
Tel: 0232 660809.

Garden sites are part of Irish history and their study affords important clues about how various social classes have expressed themselves. The Committee has initiated a broad survey of parks, gardens and demesnes which have historic interest, are sites with plant collections, or are exceptional in design or layout. An archive has been established , housed at the Historic Monuments & Buildings branch of the Department of the Environment

Book:

Northern Gardens: Gardens & Parks of Outstanding Historic Interest in Northern Ireland; 1991.

Forthcoming:

Inventory of parks, gardens and demesnes studied under a research fellowship; 1992.

NORTHERN IRELAND TOURIST BOARD

Northern Ireland Tourist Board, St Anne's Court, Belfast BT1
1ND.
Tel: 0232 231221. Fax: 0232 240960.

The protection and promotion of Northern Ireland's cultural
heritage is an important factor in the campaign to strengthen
the tourist industry and attract more visitors.

Publications:

Song of Ulster; Robbie Blair; 1988.

Visitors' Guide to Northern Ireland; Rosemary Evans; 1987.

Brochure:

Heritage of Northern Ireland; free.

Scotch Street, Armagh, by Raymond Piper from *Varieties of Britishness* (IIS)

NORTHERN VISIONS

Northern Visions Ltd, 4–8 Donegall Street Place, Belfast
BT1 2FN.
Tel: 0232 245495. Fax: 0232 326608.

The primary concern of Northern Visions is to enable local
people to become involved in telling their own stories through
the medium of video.

Videos:

Conversations at the Women's Health Fair.
> An historical document filmed at the Women's Health Fair held in
> Belfast in 1985. The camera rolls informally around the fair and
> talks to women on the stalls about their work and to the women
> who attended the workshops and stalls.

Moving Myths; Cahal McLaughlin; 1989.
> A critical look at the Protestant and Catholic institutions in
> Ireland, revealing the experiences of people who have been
> brought up in those traditions but who now regard themselves as
> atheists. Stories range from a woman sacked as a youth worker in
> Sligo because she tried to empower the young people she worked
> with to the Derry priest who left the church because he opposed its
> teachings on contraception; from the Belfast trades unionist whose
> brother died in a sectarian shooting to the woman who had to
> travel to England for an abortion.

Our Words Jump to Life; D Hyndman; 1988; (52 mins).
> 1989 Celtic Film Festival winner about young people growing up in
> Belfast: an expression of feelings and experiences through drama,
> music, poetry and photography in an epic programme which spans
> the pageantry, the celebration and the protest events in the city.

Schizophrenic City; D Hyndman; 1990; (45 mins).
> For many the 'Troubles' in Northern Ireland conjure up images of
> soldiers, bombs and sectarian violence but there is another side.
> The streets of Belfast are alive with Loyalist and Nationalist culture:
> marchers carry banners drawing on their long historical traditions.
> The arts establishment has chosen to conceal these cultural
> differences, promoting instead and ideology and view of Northern
> Ireland as a 'cosmopolitan village'. But this, the programme
> argues, ignores the true culture of the people who are determined
> to define their own identities in defence of their political
> objectives. An insider's view of the two traditions reveals a visual
> language rich in symbolism and hidden meaning spilling out into
> the streets.

Silent Story.
Plastic bullets, described by the British government as "non-lethal riot control weapons", have caused the deaths of sixteen people in Northern Ireland. This programme looks at the experiences of the relatives of the victims of plastic bullets, challenging not only the authorities' version of events (with footage of three of the events) but also the judicial and media treatment which attempt to justify the use of these deadly weapons.

Travelling People, Michael Quinn; 1991.

Under the Health Service: as Told by Belfast Women; (52 mins).
A social documentary including lively interviews with women who talk about their housing, their environment, discrimination and corruption, unemployment and poverty, the stark realities of the 'Troubles' and the future they want for their children.

Write Off; Peter Millar; 1990; (39 mins).
St Thomas' Intermediate School, located in the heart of Ballymurphy, was opened in 1957 for Catholic boys of secondary school age who were considered educational failures. It quickly developed a strong relationship with the local community. In October 1988 the school was closed by the Catholic Church without having consulted the community; the programme looks at its history and how the 'Troubles' affected it.

Forthcoming:

Amongst Ourselves; M Hyndman; 1992.
Satire.

Northern Ireland Economy; M Hyndman; 1992.

NORTHLAND

Northland Film Productions Ltd, Springrowth House, Ballinska Road, Derry BT48 0NA.
Tel: 0504 267616. Fax: 0504 363654.

Northland produces cultural and environmental heritage films for television.

Films:

Dúil sa Dúlra; BBC series; 1991; [ages 8–11]:
    Adharca agus Crúba (Goats & Deer);
    An Port Iascaireachta (The Fishing Port);
    An Seanchaisleán (the Old Norman Castle);
    An Seaniarnród (The Old Railway Line);
    Ar na hArda (In the Highlands);
    Bord na n-Éan (The Birdtable);
    Cnónna agus Caora (Nuts & Berries);
    Éanlaith an Gheimhridh (Wintering Birds);
    Faoi Scáth na gCrann (The Forest Floor).

McGilloway's Way; UTV; 1st series – 1989:
    Faughan – from Trickle to Broadmouth;
    River Faughan, County Derry – Fish & Fishers;
    Sheephaven Bay – as Far as the Ocean;
    Sheephaven Bay – Sea & Shore;
    Sperrins – Here & There, Derry, Donegal & Tyrone;
    Sperrins – Mountain Country.

McGilloway's Way; UTV; 2nd series – 1990:
    Glencolmcille – the Land's Edge;
    Glimpse of Inishowen;
    Roe Valley – in Rich Autumn;
    September in Fermanagh;
    Shoe Men & Horses;
    Winter's Tale.

McGilloway's Way; UTV; 3rd series – 1991:

>   Creeslough – Gone Fishing;

>   Fermanagh – in Among the Reed Beds;

>   Glens – County Antrim;

>   Mournes, Mist & Stone;

>   Wrecks & Racks;

>   In & around Strangford Lough.

From *Across the Foyle* (Guildhall Press)

PICTURE PRESS

Picture Press, 177 Main Street, Dundrum, Co Down BT33 0LY. Tel: 039 675 402.

Picture Press aims to provide publications which explore and question aspects of Ireland's traditional political visual imagery.

Book:

Mirrors: William III & Mother Ireland; Belinda Loftus; £9.95.
    Study of the history and impact of the visual imagery of Ireland's
    two most important symbolic figures.

Forthcoming:

Mirrors: Orange & Green; Belinda Loftus.
    The history and meaning of the symbolism associated with Orange
    parades and the nationalist tradition.

Mournes by Estyn Evans (from *Varieities of Irishness* IIS)

POOLBEG

Poolbeg Press Ltd, Knocksedan House, Forrest Great, Swords, Co Dublin.
Tel: 010 353 1 407433. Fax: 010 353 1 403753.

Poolbeg publishes books for adults and young people on literary, cultural and historical topics that are valuable resources for a cultural heritage programme.

Books:

Children of the Salmon; Eileen O'Faoláin; £3.99.

Great Northerners; Art Byrne & Sean MacMahon; 1991; £6.99.

Irish Myths & Tales; Carolyn Swift; 1990; £2.99.

Irish Sagas & Folk Tales; Eileen O'Faoláin; £4.99.

Lives; Art Byrne & Sean MacMahon; 1990; £7.99.

Poolbeg Book of Irish Ballads; Sean MacMahon; 1991; £4.99.

Poolbeg Book of Irish Heraldry; Micheál Ó Comáin; 1991; £4.99.

Poolbeg Book of Irish Placenames; Sean MacMahon; 1990; £3.99.

Rich & Rare; Sean MacMahon (ed); 1984; £7.50.

Forthcoming:

Poolbeg Book of Irish Proverbs; Fionnuala Williams; 2/92.

Taisce Duan; McMahon & O'Donoghue (eds); 2/92.

Tales of St Columba; Eileen Dunlop; 3/92.

We Are Our Past; Doreen McBride; 8/92.

THE EARL BISHOP
Frederick Hervey, Fourth Earl of Bristol
(1730-1803)
From *Lives* (Poolbeg)

PRETANI PRESS

Pretani Press, 78 Abbey Street, Bangor, Co Down BT20 4JB.
Independent publisher of books of local studies interest.

Books:

Bangor, Light of the World; Ian Adamson; £6.95.

Belfast Celtic; John Kennedy; £4.95.

Bombs on Belfast: the Blitz, 1941; £4.50.

Cavalier Duke; J C Beckett; £5.95.

Cruthin; Ian Adamson; £5.95.

Great War: a Tribute to Ulster's Heroes, 1914–18; £5.95.

Holy War in Belfast; Andrew Boyd; £4.50.

Identity of Ulster; Ian Adamson; £5.95.

Morning in Belfast; Denis Greig; £3.50.

Ulster People; Ian Adamson; £5.99.

Ulster: the Hidden History; Michael Hall; £7.50.

Diary sketch, 1915 (*All Europeans now?* IIS)

PUBLIC RECORD OFFICE

Public Record Office of Northern Ireland (PRONI), 66 Balmoral Avenue, Belfast BT9 6NY.
Tel: 0232 661621.

PRONI is the official keeper of original historical records and publisher of books, facsimiles and other printed materials.

Educational Facsimiles:

18th Century Ulster Emigration to North America; £2.40.

1798 Rebellion; £2.40.

Act of Union; £2.50.

Catholic Emancipation, 1793–1829; £1.50.

Great Famine, 1845–52; £2.40.

Ireland after the Glorious Revolution, 1692–1715; £1.50.

Irish Elections, 1750–1832; £0.45.

Penal Laws; £2.40.

Plantations in Ulster; £2.40.

Robert Emmet: the Insurrection of July 1803; £1.00.

Steps to Partition, 1885–1921; £2.40.

United Irishmen; £2.00.

Volunteers, 1778–84; £0.70.

REPLAY PRODUCTIONS

Replay Productions, Replay Theatre, Old Museum Building, 7 College Square North, Belfast BT1 6AR.
Tel: 0232 322773.

Replay uses theatre and drama workshops as a resource for the teaching of cultural heritage. The company tours schools and colleges throughout Northern Ireland with material by local writers, specially prepared to meet the needs of local children and students, and provides a full educational service which includes post-performance workshops and follow up study packs.

Study Packs:

Cow, the Ship & the Indian; Marie Jones; 1991.
    Emigration.

Permanent Deadweight; John P Rooney; 1991.
    Orphan emigration, 1849.

Forthcoming:

Hiring Days; Marie Jones; 1/92.
    Hiring fairs.

A play about alcohol abuse by Damian Gorman; 9/92.

ROYAL SOCIETY FOR THE PROTECTION OF BIRDS

Royal Society for the Protection of Birds, NI Regional Office,
Belvoir Park Forest, Belfast BT8 4QT.
Tel: 0232 491547. Fax: 0232 491669.

An appreciation of cultural heritage is enhanced by an
understanding of the natural environment in which that culture
evolved. In focusing upon birds, the RSPB education service aims
to stimulate general awareness of the environment and human
influences on the earth.

Information leaflets.

Bird table.

Feeding garden birds.

How to identify birds.

Lough Foyle.

Making bird nestboxes.

Rathlin Island.

Strangford Lough.

Treatment of sick and injured birds.

Posters:

Barn Owl; £0.50..

Birds of the Garden; £1.20..

Kingfisher; £0.50.

Osprey; £0.50.

Project Guides:

Action for Birds Project Guide; £0.75.

Bird Behaviour; £0.50.

Bird Flight; £0.50.

Bird Movement & Migration; £0.50.

Bird Studies for Primary Science in the National Curriculum; £1.25.

Bird Studies Using School Grounds; £0.75.

Birds & Estuaries; £0.50.

Birds & Mathematics in the National Curriculum; £0.75.

Birds & Their Nests; £0.50.

Birds in Art & Craft; £0.75.

Birds of Prey; £0.50.

Birds of Sea Cliff; £0.50.
    Including information on oil pollution.

Birds of Town & City; £0.50.

Conservation & Bird Protection; £0.50.
    Including information on wild birds and the law.

Environmental Games Guide; £0.75.

Feathers; £0.50.

Hedges; £0.75.

Uplands & Birds; £0.50.

Water Birds; £0.50.

Woods & Birds; ££0.50.

Resources:

Action for Birds & the Environment.
    A4 sheet.

Ban the Trade in Wild Birds.
    Set of three A5 leaflets.

Birdlife.
    Magazine for YOC members.

Birds.
    Magazine for RSPB members.

Early Birds.
    Newsletter for lower primary schools.

Focus on Birds.
    Poster for primary schools.

Sixth Sense.
    Newsletter for sixth formers.

Threats to Northern Ireland's Birds & Environment.
    A4 map.

Films and videos.

Information leaflets.

Teachers' packs.

SAINT MARY'S COLLEGE

Dr Eugene McKendry, St Mary's College, 191 Falls Road, Belfast
BT12 6FE.
Tel: 0232 327678.

The College provides support for cultural heritage, as part of the
Northern Ireland curriculum, through its pre-service,
postgraduate and in-service courses. Departments and individual
staff members carry out relevant projects and research within
their own specialist areas.

Cultural Heritage Cards:

> Lists of books and other materials to provide starting points for
> cross-curricular explorations, in the form of cards which can be
> used as bookmarks. The series is published jointly with Stranmillis
> College.

Biography as an Aspect of Cultural Heritage.

Celtic Art as an Aspect of Cultural Heritage.

Children's Fiction as an Aspect of Cultural Heritage.

Folktales & Legends as an Aspect of Cultural Heritage.

Place Names as an Aspect of Cultural Heritage.

Songs & Street Games as an Aspect of Cultural Heritage.

Resources:

Bain Sult As; Nuala Mhic Craith; secondary years 3 & 4.

EMU video and worknotes for use in secondary schools.

Fáilte.
> Irish for secondary beginners.

Foinn agus Fógrái; Séamas Ó hEiráin; GCSE.

Saothar A-Leibhéil; Liam Ó Cuinneagáin; A level.

Seal do Leasa; A level.

Seal Eile (cuid i, cuid ii); A level.

Traditional music education pack.
> Video, audio-cassette, teachers' notes, photocopy masters and OH
> transparencies.

STRANMILLIS COLLEGE/LEARNING RESOURCES UNIT

Learning Resources Unit, Stranmillis College, Belfast BT9 5DY. Tel: 0232 381271. Fax: 0232 664423.

Over the last ten years the Learning Resources Unit of Stranmillis College has been involved in the publication of educational materials, mainly concerned with local history and intended both for teachers and pupils. The provision of such material is now the unit's principal objective and the advent of the new Northern Ireland History Programme has given its task added impetus and urgency.

Books for Teachers:

Growing up in Northern Ireland; J Harbison (ed); £6.95.

Irish Scientists & Technologists: Cultural Heritage through History & Science in the Primary School; J Emberson and P Pilson; £1.20.

Teaching History to Slow Learning Children in Secondary Schools; C V McIver (ed); £4.48.

Cultural Heritage Cards:

Lists of books and other materials to provide starting points for cross-curricular explorations, in the form of cards which can be used as bookmarks. The series is published jointly with Saint Mary's College.

Biography as an Aspect of Cultural Heritage.

Celtic Art as an Aspect of Cultural Heritage.

Children's Fiction as an Aspect of Cultural Heritage.

Folktales & Legends as an Aspect of Cultural Heritage.

Place Names as an Aspect of Cultural Heritage.

Songs & Street Games as an Aspect of Cultural Heritage.

Publications for Primary Pupils (Key Stage 1):

Long Ago and Far Away; £1.20.

Long Ago in Ireland; £1.20.

Publications for Primary Pupils (Key Stage 2):

Farm in 1900; £0.80.

Home in 1900; £0.80.

Leisure in 1900; (with 'Mummers: a Resource Booklet for Teachers' prepared by the Ulster-American Folk Park); £0.80.

School in 1900; £0.80.

Settlers in Ireland: Archaeology & Evidence; (introductory book); £1.50.

Street in 1900; £0.80.

Transport in 1900; £0.80.

Publications for Lower Secondary Pupils:

Christianity in Downpatrick & Lecale; (with teachers' notes); £1,00.

Search in Evidence; (two units plus teachers' notes); £50.00 (class set of thirty).

Search in Time; (three units plus teacher' notes); £35.00 (class set of thirty).

Videos (for secondary schools):

Grey Abbey; £10.00.

Nendrum; £10.00.

Norman Castle in Ulster; £18.00.

Saint Patrick: the Myth & the Reality; £18.00.

Ulster at War, 1914–18; £40.00 (four tapes).

STRANMILLIS COLLEGE/RELIGIOUS STUDIES

Department of Religious Studies, Stranmillis College, Stranmillis Road, Belfast BT9 5DY.
Tel: 0232 381271.

The Department has a professional interest in training students and teachers to teach about religious and cultural traditions within, and beyond, the Northern Ireland community.

Book:

Small World: a Handbook on Introducing World Religions in the Primary School; Maurice Ryan; 1988; [ages 5–11 and teachers].
Includes detailed accounts of the history, organisation and activities of the Chinese, Indian, Jewish and Muslim communities in Northern Ireland.

From *Small World*

ULSTER ARCHITECTURAL HERITAGE SOCIETY

Ulster Architectural Heritage Society, 181a Stranmillis Road, Belfast BT9 5DU.
Tel: 0232 660809.

The interests of the Ulster Architectural Society extend, in time, from the very earliest structures, through those of the Georgian and Victorian periods, to the very latest in contemporary architecture; and, in space, throughout the nine counties of the province of Ulster. Its objects are: to promote the appreciation and enjoyment of good architecture of all periods; to encourage the preservation of buildings and groups of artistic merit or historic importance; and to encourage public awareness and appreciation of the beauty, history and character of local neighbourhoods.

Books, Monographs and Essays:

Architectural Schizophrenia; £1.60.

Ballywalter Park; £2.50.

Clandeboye; £3.00.

Classical Churches in Ulster, £1.60.

Fishmongers' Company in Ulster; £4.80.

Introduction to Modern Ulster Architecture; £4.00.

Introduction to Ulster Architecture; £4.00.

Irish Church Monuments, 1570–1880; £3.00.

J J McCarthy & the Gothic Revival in Ireland; £3.00.

Malone House; £1.20.

Mausolea in Ulster; £1.00.

Moneymore & Draperstown; £4.00

Palm House & Botanic Gardens in Belfast; £2.00.

Roger Mulholland, Architect of Belfast; £0.80.

Workhouses of Ulster; £1.60.

Lists and surveys:

Banbridge; £1.60.

Carrickfergus; £2.00.

Craigavon (omnibus volume); £2.00.

Donaghadee & Portpatrick; £3.00.

Dungannon & Cookstown; £2.00.

Island of Rathlin; £1.40.

Joy Street area of Belfast; £1.20.

Malone & Stranmillis; £7.50.

North Antrim; £2.40.

Queen's University area of Belfast (1975); £2.40.

Rathfriland & Hilltown; £1.40.

Town of Cavan; £1.80.

Town of Monaghan; £1.80.

Towns & villages of mid Down; £2.40.

West Antrim; £1.20.

ULSTER FOLK & TRANSPORT MUSEUM

Ulster Folk & Transport Museum, Cultra, Holywood, Co Down
BT18 0EU.
Tel: 0232 428428.

The Ulster Folk and Transport Museum is one of the most
important centres for the study of our social history and cultural
heritage. It offers unique opportunities to teachers wishing to
fulfil the requirements of the New Curriculum with respect to
Cross-Curricular Themes, especially Cultural Heritage and
Education for Mutual Understanding. Teachers seeking advice
or assistance in these areas are most welcome to contact the
museum's Education Department. To aid teachers and students
in their studies, the museum has, in recent years, embarked on a
major publishing programme to provide material of specific
local reference.

Booklets:

Brotherhoods in Ireland; £3.75.
  Traces the origins and development of the Buffaloes, Foresters,
  Freemasons, Knights of Columbanus, Odd Fellows, Orangemen
  and Rechabites.

Collecting Oral History; £1.00.
  An essential handbook for anyone interested in collecting oral
  history.

Flute in Ireland; £1.20.
  The history and development of the flute, its players and its place
  in our cultural heritage.

Giant's Causeway, Portrush & Bush Valley Railway & Tramway Co Ltd;
  £1.20.
  A short, illustrated history of the famous line which pioneered the
  use of hydro-electricity to power railways.

Renascence of the Irish Art of Lacemaking; £1.20.
  A facsimile reprint of a work first published in 1888, with a new
  introduction.

Ulster Needlework – A Continuing Tradition; £3.95.
  A brief history of Irish embroidery and patchwork, with full colour
  illustrations.

Books:

English Dialects of Ulster.
> Published in memory of the late G B Adams, Dialectic Archivist at the museum from 1964 to 1982 and including his most significant articles.

Use of Tradition; £9.95.
> Essays presented by friends and colleagues to George Thompson, first Director of the museum.

Educational Materials:

Activity Guide; £0.95; [UP/LS].
> Written by Education Department staff and published for the museum by Longmans, this lavishly illustrated booklet offers the younger visitor an interesting and educational guide to their visit, with exercises for visit, school and home.

At School 100 Years Ago; £2.50; [UP/LS].
> Pack for teachers who wish to recreate a typical school day of the 1890s in the Ballydown National School. Full instructions included (with ideas for adapting modern address to simulate historical costume) and a brief history of the national school system, with lessons which may be photocopied.

Crafted in Ireland; £3.50.
> A lavishly illustrated look at some thirty crafts once common throughout Ireland.

Design Story of the Bicycle; £3.00 (class sets £2.50 each); [US].
> The evolution of the bicycle and its social impact seen from the viewpoint of design and technological advances. Intended primarily for CDT classes but also useful for historical studies.

Edwardian Belfast; £3.00; [US].
> A source pack on aspects of life in Belfast in Edwardian times, designed for A-Level History studies. Also very useful reference for project work and local studies at other levels and can be used in conjunction with the 'Titanic' pack.

Illustrations of the Irish Linen Industry; £0.75.
> In 1783 William Hincks produced a series of engravings illustrating the production of linen, from the ploughing o' the land to sow the flax seed to selling the finished cloth. This booklet contains all twelve illustrations with detailed commentary on each one.

Irish Linen Industry; £2.00.
> A brief, well illustrated history of the processes and development of the industry covering many aspects of production and

marketing, the uses of technology and modern developments. Published in association with the Irish Linen Guild.

Linen: Continuity & Change; £3.00 (class sets £2.50 each); [LS/US]. An 8–10 week course for third year secondary pupils on linen in Ulster: the domestic industry, the processing of flax into linen, industrialisation, working in the linen mills and factories, living and working in a mill village (a case study of Bessbrook) and the decline and renasence of the industry. Published in association with the Irish Linen Guild.

National Schools, 1831–1921; £3.00 (class sets £2.50 each); [LS]. Unit of work (8–10 weeks) for first year secondary pupils which uses a wide variety of primary sources, photographs etc to build up a comprehensive picture of the Irish national school system – an educational system so successful that it was copied completely in New South Wales in the nineteenth century. This can be a teacher's handbook for younger classes.

Patchwork Bedcovers; £20.00. A tape/slide pack, with notes, illustrating aspects of folk art and social history.

Railway Age in Ireland; £3.00 (class sets £2.00 each); [LS] The development of railways had an enormous impact on Irish society in the nineteenth and early twentieth centuries. This unit of work for second year secondary pupils traces the history and development of Irish railways and examines their effect on society. Published in association with Northern Ireland Railways.

Titanic – An Education Pack; £3.00 (class sets £2.50 each); [LS/US]. An 8–10 week course of study intended for third year secondary pupils but also widely used for GCSE History coursework. The material examines the period (early 1900s), the vessel's construction, the voyage and the disaster and its aftermath. Selected by the South Australia Education Authority for use in its schools.

Ulster Farming & Food; £2.50 (class sets £2.00 each); [UP/LS]. Unit of work on the farming industry in Ulster, past and present. Includes elementary biology, chemistry, meteorology and studies of diet, as well as an examination of crops, livestock, the natural cycle and the farmer's year.

Ulster Farming from Old Photographs; £2.50. A collection of old photographs from the museum's archives which illustrate the main farming activities of the early years of this century.

Ulster Folk Ways; £2.95.
> An overview of the museum's collections, setting them in their historical context. Well illustrated in both colour and black and white; published by Eason & Son Ltd (no 20 in their Irish Heritage series).

White Star Line; £2.00.
> A facsimile of the booklet published in 1911 to publicise the new liners, Olympic and Titanic.

Nature Study Booklets:

> The museum's grounds offer primary pupils an excellent environment for nature study. Teachers wishing to use these booklets with their classes are advised to 'walk the route' before the visit, to survey it and make themselves aware of the demands of the terrain.

Flower Power; £1.25.
> An introduction to the study of flowers and plants.

Animal Tracks; £1.95.
> A look at some of the wild animals which live in the museum grounds.

Woodland Trail; £1.95.
> A look at the plants, trees and flowers in their natural environment.

Periodical:

Ulster Folklife; volumes 4, 5 and 7 (£1.00 each), 11 and 14 (reprints at £3.00), 18, 21 and 23 (£2.00), 22, 24 and 25 (£3.00), 26 (£4.00), 27–31 (£5.00), 32 and 33 (£6.00) and 34–37 are available. The museum's annual research journal.

Resources:

Audio Archive.
> Recordings of interviews with correspondents on different aspects of life in the past, folk tales, stories and music. It is essential to make arrangements with the Audio Archivist prior to consultation.

BBC Archive.
> BBC Northern Ireland has placed its radio archive in the museum to ensure its preservation. Most of the material relates to broadcasts from the 1960s onwards and is presently being catalogued. Prior arrangement for consultation is essential.

Harland & Wolff Photographic Archive.
   An unrivalled resource for the study of shipbuilding, local industry
   and technological progress.

Library.
   Holding over 20,000 books as well as journals, magazines and
   archival material, the museum library is open for public
   consultation during office hours. It is recommended that
   arrangements are made with the librarian, prior to making a visit.

W A Green Photographic Collection.
   Over 4,000 photographs taken mainly between 1910 and 1925,
   constituting an invaluable resource for the study of rural life,
   crafts, farming and domestic industry.

Trails:

Ballyveridagh National School.

Coshkib Hill Farm.

Let's Look at Corradreenan.

Lets Look at Lismacloskey.

Let's Look at Tea Lane.

On the Flax Trail.
   Simple worksheets on buildings in the open-air museum. One set
   free to teachers, class sets may be photocopied [UP/LS].

Videos:

Ring of Cultra; 28 mins; available on loan; [LP/UP].
   A fairy story about two children and a magic ring, designed to
   introduce younger children to the museum before their visit.

Linen Industry; 12 mins; available on loan; [UP/LS].
   A look at the processes of long ago, contrasting them with modern
   techniques.

Farming & Food; 15 mins; available on loan; [UP/LS].
   A look at the old-style farming methods still used at the museum.
   Includes farmwork with horses and various methods of harvesting
   by hand and simple machine.

Pothooks Not Spiders; 28 mins; may be viewed at the museum only; [LP/
   UP/LS].
   A composite version of two BBC schools programmes in the Green
   Peas and Barley-O series – 'At Home in 1917' and 'At School in
   1917' – which were filmed in the museum. The film follows a day

in the life of James Gillespie from early morning to the end of the school day.

Caterpillar Trail; 15 mins; may be viewed at the museum only; [LP/UP].
A programme from the BBC series, made at the museum. Children see bread being made in the traditional way and learn about farm animals and travel by horse and cart.

Dusty Bluebells; may be viewed at the museum only.
Children's street games in 1960s Belfast.

Wee Blue Blossom; may be viewed at the museum only.
1950s (b&w) film of the linen industry.

Hands; may be viewed at the museum only.
Series of 30 mins films of traditional crafts: 'Bees & Bee Skeps', 'Carley Bridge Potter', 'Cavan Cooper', 'Cavan Inlay Craftsman', 'Dublin Candlemaker', 'Irish Lace', 'Rushwork', 'Shoemaker' and 'Stonemason'.

Dairy artefacts from *A journey into the past* (Ulster American Folk Park)

ULSTER HISTORICAL FOUNDATION

Ulster Historical Foundation, 12 College Square East, Belfast BT1 6DD.
Tel: 0232 681365.

The Foundation is concerned with genealogical research and publishing: guides to sources for family historians and material of general relevance for the history of Ireland, with special emphasis on emigration.

Books:

Heart of Down: Old Banbridge Families from Gravestone Inscriptions, Wills & Biographical Notes; R S J Clarke; 1989.

Making Sense of History: Evidence in Ireland for the Young Historian; Parkhill, Gallagher and Kinealy (eds); 1990; [ages 12–16].

Scottish Migration to Ulster in the Reign of James I; M Perceval-Maxwell; 1990 (new ed). They Wrought Among the Tow: Flax & Linen in Co Tyrone, 1750–1900; Pat MacDonnell; 1990; [GCSE].

Ulster Politics: the Formative Years, 1868–86; B M Walker; 1990.

Forthcoming:

Autobiography of a Belfast Working Man: Robert McElborough.

Funeral Register of the First Presbyterian Church of Belfast; spring/92.

Guild Subscribers' Interest List No 14; 12/91.

Land & Politics in Ulster; 12/92.

Life in Linenopolis: the Memoirs of William Topping, Belfast Damask Weaver, 1903–56; 12/91.

Merchants in Plenty: Joseph Smyth's Directories of Belfast, 1807/8; 12/92.

Nine Ulster Lives; 3/92.

Northern Nationalism, Partition & the Catholic Minority, c1890–1929; spring/92.

Old Belfast Families: Clifton Street Gravestone Inscriptions; 12/91.

Old Downpatrick Families: Co Down Gravestone Inscriptions; Vol 7 – 3/92 (new ed).

Presbyterians & the Irish Language; summer/92.

That Elusive Irish Ancestor; summer/92.
　　Selection of conference papers.

Victorian Belfast; spring/92.

GENEALOGICAL RESEARCH ~ PUBLICATIONS ~ LECTURE TOURS ~ IRISH GENEALOGICAL PROJECT

**ULSTER
HISTORICAL
FOUNDATION**
~ESTABLISHED 1956 ~

ULSTER HISTORY PARK

The Ulster History Park, Cullion, Omagh, Co Tyrone BT79 7SU.
Tel: 06626 48188.
The aim of the Ulster History Park is to portray as accurately and
as comprehensively as possible the settlement history of Ireland,
from the Stone Age to the end of the 17th century.

Resource Packs:

Early Christian Ireland.

Life in Early Times.

Normans in Ireland.

Vikings.

Trail workbooks of the Ulster History Park.

Resource Packs Forthcoming:

16th & 17th Century Ireland; 1993.

Castles & Fortifications; 1993.

Services:

Audio-visual theatre, library and education resource room for use of
visiting school groups. Interactive computers to reinforce learning
through use of IT.

ULSTER MUSEUM

Ulster Museum, Botanic Gardens, Belfast BT9 5AB.
Tel: 0232 381251. Fax: 0232 665510.

The primary objective of the Ulster Museum is to increase the public's understanding of our heritage by collecting, exhibiting, preserving and studying objects of interest in the fields of archaeology, art, history, industry, natural history, science and sociology. The material produced by the museum is directed towards the achievement of this objective and is an important resource for every level of the formal education system, for formal and informal adult and community education programmes, and for the general public.

Cards and Postcards:

Antiquities series; colour; £0.10 each.

Armada in Ireland series; colour; £0.05 or £0.10 each.

Art works series; colour; £0.10 each.

Béal Feirste to Belfast series; black & white/colour; £0.25 each.

Hogg photographs; sepia; £0.10 each.

Kings in Conflict series: Ireland in the 1690s; colour; £0.10 each.

Local history series; colour; £0.10 each.

Photographs:

Belfast.

Hogg Collection.

Welch Collection.

Posters:

Battle of the Boyne; £2.50.

Cities Besieged; £0.50.

From Béal Feirste to Belfast; £0.95.

Kings in Conflict; £0.50.

William Petty's Map of Ireland in 1690; £3.50.

Prints:

McKelvey watercolours of old Belfast.

Paintings of William Conor.

Various Ulster scenes.

Publications:

Armada Package; £1.50 each.

    Archaeology: Life on Board.

    Armada in Ireland.

    Armada at Sea','Guns & Gunnery.

Belfast: Site & City; £1.95.

Changing Face of Belfast; £0.95.

Early Irish Ironworking; £19.95/£25.00.

Girona; £0.25.

    Treasures from the Girona Collection.

Ireland's Armada Legacy; £9.95.

    Includes a catalogue of the museum's Armada Collection.

Irish Tower Houses; £0.05

Spinning Wheels: the John Horner Collection; £0.15.

Welch Collection I; £0.50.

    A list of Welch's topography and history photographs.

Welch Collection II; £0.50.

    A list of Welch's botany, geology and zoology photographs.

Slide pack:

Treasures of the Spanish Armada; £9.20.

    A general set of twenty coloured slides, mainly of objects recovered from Spanish ships wrecked off the Irish coast. Various topics are illustrated: events in the English Channel, the return voyage and the wreck of the Girona near the Giant's Causeway. Illustrations of guns and gunnery and navigation equipment are included. for primary pupils the pack can be used in conjunction with 'The Spanish Armada' by Sheela Speers (pub Ladybird Books) whilst for post-primary levels David Anderson's book of the same title (pub MacDonald) is invaluable.

100

Forthcoming Video:

Belfast Times; 1/92.

Two young people investigate aspects of life in and around Belfast in early times; the sixteenth, seventeenth and eighteenth centuries; Victorian times; and the present day. It will be appropriate for KS2 History core units and Local Studies at KS2 and KS3, including environmental issues with Geography teaching in mind. Extensive notes are to be included and copies of historic maps of the city and a slide pack will be available. The video will be complemented by an education pack from the Belfast Development Office, which will include pupils' work booklets, teachers' notes, additional source and worksheets, and a database on Victorian National School rolls.

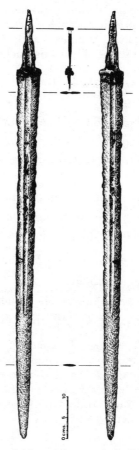

Drawing by Deirdre Crone of thirteenth century Polish sword found int he river Blackwater (from *All Europeans now?* IIS)

ULSTER PEOPLE'S COLLEGE

Ulster People's College, 30 Adelaide Park, Belfast. BT9 6FY.

The People's College aims to help the two communities in Northern Ireland to understand and appreciate the traditions of the other and to provide a basis for self-knowledge.

Book:

Working Class Community in Northern Ireland; Peter McNamee & Tom Lovett; 1987; £7.50.
An attempt to give working class people from all over Northern Ireland – men, women, young people, Catholics and Protestants – a voice to discuss the social and economic issues and the cultural, political and moral pressures which exert an overwhelming influence over their lives. As an educational aid, the book can be used alone or with a series of learning packs based upon its five sections.

Resources:

Community education & division seminar report; £1.00.

Oral history manual; £1.50.

People's history conference report; £1.00.

Information Packs:

Community & Environment; Peter McNamee; 1989; £2.50.

Links between People; Peter McNamee; 1989.

Northern Ireland: the Two Traditions; Peter McNamee; 1989; £2.50.

Oral History; Peter McNamee; 1989.

Women in the Community; Peter McNamee; 1989; £1.50.

Work & Unemployment; Peter McNamee; 1989; £1.50.

ULSTER PLACE-NAME SOCIETY

The Treasurer, Ulster Place-Name Society, Celtic Department, The Queen's University of Belfast, Belfast BT7 11N.

The Society studies the origin, history, use and development of personal and place names in Ireland and other Celtic countries.

Journal:

Ainm; Ruairí Ó hUiginn (ed); annually from 1986.

INVESTIGATING
PLACE NAMES
——IN——
ULSTER

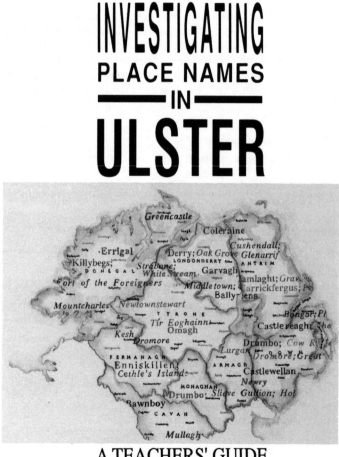

A TEACHERS' GUIDE
By Jonathan Bardon

ULSTER QUAKER PEACE EDUCATION PROJECT

Ulster Quaker Peace Education Project, Magee College, University of Ulster, Londonderry BT48 7JL.

The Peace Education Project offers a teacher support role, addressing issues of diversity, prejudice and conflict. Provides a team of skilled, trained facilitators to lead workshops for all ages in classrooms or in joint school ventures. Also able to facilitate alliance building exercises that tackle contentious issues in a constructive way.

Book:

Prejudice Reduction Workshop Approach; Will Peget; 1991; [6th form & adult].

Forthcoming:

Wee People; Eileen Healy; 1992; [P & LS].
    Conflict resolution skills.

ULSTER SOCIETY

The Ulster Society, Brownlow House, Windsor Avenue, Lurgan, Co Armagh BT67 9BJ.

The Society aims to promote the rich heritage and culture of the Ulster-British people through books, exhibitions, lectures and excursions.

Books:

Life-Line to Freedom: Ulster in the Second World War; Derrick Gibson-Harries; 1990.

Pardon Me Boy: the Americans in Ulster, 1942–45; Ronnie Hanna; 1991. A pictorial record.

Never Call Retreat: the Life & Times of Ulysses S Grant, Ulster-American Hero; Ronnie Hanna; 1991; £5.95.

Ulster Covenant: a Pictorial Record of the 1912 Home Rule Crisis; Gordon Lucy; 1989.

William Johnston of Ballykilbeg; Aiken McClelland; 1991.

Forthcoming:

Land of the Free: Ulster & the American Revolution; Ronnie Hanna; 5/92.

ULSTER TELEVISION

Ulster Television plc, Havelock House, Ormeau Road, Belfast
BT7 1EB.
Tel: 0232 328122. Fax: 0232 246695.

UTV is an independent regional television company making and
commissioning local programmes for transmission in Northern
Ireland.

Programmes:

Belfast Trilogy:

    Loving Look at Belfast; Janthia Duncan; 1991.

    Goodbye Old Flame; John Scobbie & John Marley; 1991.

    Pass; Rory Fitzpatrick; 1991.

Facing the Future; Desmond Bell; 1991.

    Derry.

Fiddles & Flutes; Michael Beattie & Steve Ward; 1990.

Once Upon a Place; Janthia Duncan; 1990.

Forthcoming:

Derry Trilogy:

    Far Frontiers; 1992.

    Once upon a Place; 1992.

ULSTER WILDLIFE TRUST

Education Officer, Ulster Wildlife Trust, Ulster Wildlife Centre, 3 New Line, Killyleagh Road, Crossgar, Co Down BT30 9EP. Tel: 0396 830282.

The Trust is a charity dedicated to the conservation of the wildlife and natural habitats of Northern Ireland.

Resources:

Conservation Education Pack for Schools; £5.00 + £1.00 p&p.
> A teaching pack for schools, full of practical ideas for conservation activities in and around the school grounds.

Wildlife Gardening Handbook; £3.95 + £0.50 p&p.
> An eighty page handbook for wildlife gardening: ponds, trees and shrubs, bird and bat boxes, hedges etc.

ULSTER-AMERICAN FOLK PARK

Education Officer, Ulster-American Folk Park, Camphill, Omagh, Co Tyrone BT78 5QY.

The Folk Park is a reconstruction of emigration history and the emigrant experience showing rural life and crafts in 19th century Ulster, seasonal customs and amusements, village crafts and a 19th century shop.

Books:

Mellon House; 1981.

How It All Began; Eric Montgomery; 1991.

Scotch-Irish & Ulster; Eric Montgomery; 1971.

Selected Ulster & American 19th Century Farmhouse Recipes; 1989.

Thomas Mellon & His Times; Thomas Mellon; 1976.

Teaching/Information Packs:

Across the Atlantic; 1989.

    Emigration.

Activity Pack for Slow Learning Secondary Pupils; 1987.

Barn Dancing; 1990.

Discovering the Ulster-American Folk Park; 1986.

Journey into the Past; 1986.

Mummers; 1991.

Study leaflets.

    Set of eleven.

Trail for Tiny Tots; 1988.

    Rural Ulster.

Forthcoming:

Pennsylvania Frontier; 1993; [ages 11–14].

ULTACH TRUST

Ultach Trust, 17 Castle Arcade, Belfast BT1 5DG.
Tel: 0232 230749. Fax: 0232 321245.

The Trust aims to widen appreciation of the contribution made
by the Irish language to the culture of Northern Ireland and to
increase knowledge of the language throughout all sections of
the community. It's objectives include promotion of the
language in Northern Ireland, acting as a funding agency, and
liaising with relevant public and voluntary bodies. It is happy to
advise on all aspects of the Irish language and its Trustees reflect
a wide spectrum of interests and viewpoints.

Book:

Introduction to the Irish Language; William Neilson; 1808, reprinted 1990;
£6.50.
Most important record of Co Down Irish, recorded by a
Presbyterian minister and native speaker. The bilingual dialogues
included are a valuable source for social historians.

Information Leaflet:

Protestant Gaelic Tradition; Aodán Mac Póilin; 1990; free.
Describes Protestant involvement in Irish from the 17th to 19th
centuries.

Forthcoming Publications:

Irish-Medium Education in Northern Ireland: a Report; Aodán Mac Póilin;
1992.

Pronouncing Irish Names: a Courtesy Guide; Róise Ní Bhaoill; 1992.
Will help those who find difficulty with names in the Irish
language and wish to pronounce them with greater accuracy.

Scéalta Oirghialla/Tales from Oriel; Seosamh Laoide, edited by Seán Ó
Coinn ; 1992.
Folktales recorded from Irish speakers in Armagh, Monaghan,
Omeath and Meath at the turn of the century.

Tale of Deirdre; Samuel Bryson, edited by Breandán Ó Buachalla & Róise
Ní Bhaoill; 1992.

WHITE ROW PRESS

White Row Press, 135 Cumberland Road, Dundonald, Belfast BT16 0BB.
Tel: 0232 482586.

White Row Press is an independent publisher of a range of local studies books, some of which are reprints.

Books:

Big Wind; Peter Carr; 1991.
　　The legendary 'Big Wind' of 1839.

Blackmouth & Dissenter; John Monteith Barkley; 1991.
　　Autobiography of the Presbyterian radical.

Gape Row; Agnes Romilly White; 1934, reprinted 1988.
　　Vernacular comedy set in a rural Ulster village on the eve of the First World War.

Most Unpretending of Places; Peter Carr; 1987.
　　History of Dundonald, Co Down.

Mrs Murphy Buries the Hatchet; Agnes Romilly White; 1936, reprinted 1989.
　　Sequel to Gape Row.

Two Centuries of Life in Down, 1600–1800; John Stevenson; 1920, reprinted 1990.

Yes Matron; Peggy Donaldson; 1989.
　　History of nurses and nursing at the Royal Victoria Hospital, Belfast.

WORKERS' EDUCATIONAL ASSOCIATION

Workers' Educational Association, 1 Fitzwilliam Street, Belfast
BT9 6AW.
Tel: 0232 329718.

As a voluntary body which specialises in political education and
community participation, the WEA is keen to foster ventures
which increase mutual understanding between the two traditions
in Northern Ireland and to work with those who are trying to
combat sectarianism.

Books:

Stop at the Tramway Bridge; Carrickfergus WEA Oral History Class; £3.95.

Dander Down the Streets; Kilmacormick WEA History Group; £3.95.
   Memories of life in the old backstreets community of Enniskillen.

My Own Place; £1.50.
   Writing about the Ards by local people, prepared in partnership
   with the Northern Ireland Arts Council and other sponsors.

Writer to Writer; Sam Burnside; £1.50.
   WEA Studies in Community Education, No 1.

Working with the Unemployed; Mark Robinson, £1.00.
   WEA Studies in Community Education, No 2.

Lost Horizons, New Horizons: Community Development in Northern Ireland.
   Papers from the conference on community development held at
   Magee College, November 1988.

Training & Arts Administration in Northern Ireland; Sam Burnside; £1.50.

Leaflets:

Flowerfield Arts Centre: WEA courses in Coleraine.

Interface: towards an anti-sectarian future.

Link into Learning: community education in Belfast.

Reportback: WEA review, Spring 1991.

WEA Annual Report: 1990–91.

WEA: what it is and what it does.

WRITING INTO READING PROJECT

Writing Into Reading Project, Deramore High School, Carolan Road, Belfast BT7 3HE.
Tel: 0232 692411.

Writing Into reading is a cross-curricular project which aims to provide a body of regional material for primary and secondary schools, written by pupils, teachers and parents; each school is seen as a unit for curriculum design. The material listed will be on view at Deramore High School. from January to April 1992.

Materials Designed by Parents:

Tales from Bushmills:
  Keefe.
  Trap.
  Victor the Viking.

Tales from Killyclogher:
  Colton's Hill.
  Now You See It; a play.
  Tree House.

Tales from Mourne.
  Translated into French and Irish and presented in English in colour comic form.

Tales from Portadown:
  Christmas Tree.
  Duck That Flew Away.
  Selshion Moss.

Tales from Strabane:
  Barney the Mill Mouse.
  Fire down the Canal.
  Unexpected Dip.
  Tales from the Creggan.

Materials Designed by Pupils (Lower Primary):

Cutting Turf.

Games of Sandymount.

Giant's Causeway.

Home Life in the Past.

Local Birds.
   Mourne.

Sandymount Snails.

Materials Designed by Pupils (Upper Primary):

Burren.

Dundonald Dot.

Electricity in Donaghadee.

Fairy Cobbler.

Photographs of Dalkey & Strabane.

Sheep Farming, Glencorp.

Skateboarding.

Wellworth's Werewolf.

Materials Designed by Teachers:

Aerodrome, Ardboe.

Connor & Lucky.
   River Bush.

Lough Neagh.

Tales from Omagh.

Materials Designed by the Project:

Awkward Pass; [ages 10–12].
   A play about Cuchulain and Maeve.

Going to Belfast in the 19th Century; [ages 10–12].
   The language, vocabulary and accent of the city in an historical
   setting.

Lying Brian; [ages 10–12].
   A play.

Second Storey; [ages 10–12].
   Belfast boys add a second storey to their gang hut.

Three Dialect Poets; [GCSE].
   An introduction to three poets writing in the 18th and 19th
   centuries.

Three Folk Tales; [ages 10–12].
   Colour comic.

Ulster Speech.
　　A booklet for teachers on vocabulary and accent.

Forthcoming (Designed by the Project):

Folk Tales of Ulster.

Plays about St Patrick.

Interior of a national school, from *The Printed Word on the Common Man* IIS

YES! PUBLICATIONS

Yes! Publications, Holywell House, 32 Shipquay Street, Derry BT48 6DW.
Tel: 0504 363729.

Yes! aims to give ordinary people living in the north-west the opportunity to publish material which is of interest to their local communities and is generally neglected by larger, more commercially oriented publishers. The ongoing Blueprint Project is recording the hopes, fears and expectations of twelve local young people as they approach the twenty-first century.

Books:

Down the Quay: a Photographic Record of Derry Dockers, 1945–90; John Coyle; 1990.

History of the Old Waterside; Ernest Tacey; 1991.

Rosemount: a Village & a School; Hugh Gallagher et al; 1991.

Spectator & Other Derry Stories; Hugh Gallagher; 1990.
Anthology of short stories whose theme is growing up in Derry in the '50s and '60s.

Three Cheers for the Derrys; Gardiner S Mitchell; 1991.
History of the Derry regiments which fought in World War One.

Voices over the Wall; 5th Form pupils of St Columb's College, Derry; 1991.
Anthology of short stories.

Journal:

Fingerpost; Eamonn Deane (ed).
Quarterly magazine dealing with issues affecting the local community.

Forthcoming History Topics:

Derry railways.

Foyle Harps football team.

Shirt factories.

MISCELLANEOUS

Booklist:

Cultural Heritage/Education for Mutual Understanding.
Compiled for the EMU Conference/DENI Summer School 1990.
Extensive titles list for KS3 and KS4, covering a wide range of
subject areas.

Books:

Acts of Union; Desmond Bell; Macmillan.

As the Crow Flies over Rough Terrain; James G Kenny; Styletype Printing,
Belfast; 1988.

Ballymoney & District, Prior to the 20th Century; J B Hamilton; J S Scarlett;
1957.

Belleek: a Community & Visitors' Guide; Belleek Community Association.

*Caring by Design: the Architectural Heritage of the Health & Social Services in
Northern Ireland*; Cahal Dallat; Department of Health & Social
Services; 1985.

Castle Caldwell; John Cunningham.

Culture & Anarchy in Ireland, 1890–1939; F S L Lyons; Oxford University
Press.

Culture & Politics in Northern Ireland; G Hughes (ed); Open University
Press.

Dunloy Past & Present; Mary McLean; 1990.

Far from Owenreagh: Memories of John Graham, 1899–1983; G Mawhinney,
Labby, Draperstown, Co Londonderry BT45 7BG.
An emigrant to Australia recalls his varied life.

Fermanagh Lakeland; Walter Brady.

Fermanagh Story; Peadar Livingstone.

God Save Ulster; Steve Bruce; Oxford University Press.

Harsh Winds of Rathlin; Tommy Cecil; Impact Printing; 1990.

History of Magherafelt; W H Maitland; G Mawhinney, Labby,
Draperstown, Co Londonderry BT45 7BG.

Ireland's Cultural Heritage in Words & Music; Elizabeth Quinn & Doreen
McBride; B Q Publications, 13 Ardis Avenue, Lisburn, Co Antrim
BT28 3PX; 1991.

Ireland: A Social & Cultural History, 1922–85; Terence Brown; Fontana.

Ireland: A Sociological Profile; Sociological Association of Ireland.

Irish Emigration Lists, 1833–39; Brian Mitchell; Genealogical Centre, 10 Bishop Street , Derry BT48 6PW.

Irish Folkways; E Estyn Evans; Routledge & Kegan Paul.

Irish Heritage; E Estyn Evans; Dundalgan Press.

Living by Lough Erne; Mary Rogers.

Looking Back on Ballinascreen; Angela J O'Keeney; Author, 7 Tobermore Road, Draperstown, Co Londonderry BT45 7AG.

Mysterious Boa Island; John Cunningham.

Nationalist & Unionist Ireland; David Gray; Blackie.

On the Shining Bann: Records of an Ulster Manor; R M Sibbett; Braid Books, 69 Galgorm Road, Ballymena, Co Antrim BT42 1AA. Facsimile reprint of 1928 edition.

Pain & Pleasure: Rathmoyle Reminiscences; Faith Gibson & Sue Towers; Northern Health & Social Services Board; 1990.

Parishes of Devenish & Boho ; George Elliott.

Pauper to Patient: History of the Route Hospital, BBallymoney; Cecil Burns; Impact Printing; 1988.

Prospect of Tyrone; Mary Rogers.

Recall; Samuel Foster.
History of Orangeism in Fermanagh.

Rooms of Time: Memories of Ulster Folk; Cahal Dallat & Faith Gibson; Department of Health & Social Services; 1988.

Shamrock; Charles Nelson; Boethius Press.

Ulsterheart; C Brett Ingram; All Ireland Heritage Inc.

Waybridge: the Life & Times of Mary Crawford, 1895–1990; Maureen McGauran; Author, 41 Hillhead Crescent, Belfast BT11 9FS: 1991.

Welcome Back to Mullanaskea; Topped Mountain Historical Society.
Story of Mullanaskea School.

Bookshops:

Bookworm Community Bookshop, 16 Bishop Street, Derry BT48 6PW. Tel: 0504 261616.
Libraries and schools supplier; mail order service available.

Dillons, 44–46 Fountain Street, Belfast. Tel: 0232 240159.
Good stock of Irish material.

Emerald Isle Books, 539 Antrim Road, Belfast BT15 3BU.
Tel: 0232 370798.
> Extensive stock of secondhand books of Irish interest,covering a wide range of subjects.

L W N Hall, 10 High Street, Enniskillen, Co Fermanagh.
Tel: 0365 324341.
> Good stock of local studies books.

University Book Shop Ltd, Academic & General Booksellers,
91 University Road, Belfast BT7 1NL.
Tel: 0232 666302/662552.
> As well as stocking an extensive selection of of academic books, the University Book Shop provides a full general service for the community as a whole. Many of the 50,000 titles in stock concern Irish history, politics and literature. A mail order facility is available.

Waterstones, 8 Royal Avenue, Belfast.
Tel: 0232 247355.
> Good stock of Irish material.

Information Pack:

Leslie Hill Historic Farm & Park, Ballymoney.

Journals:

Banbridge & District Historical Society Journal.

Bangor Historical Society Journal.

Donegal Annual; Donegal Historical Society.

Down Rail; Downpatrick Railway Society.

Dromore & District Local Historical Group Journal.

Dufferin Chronicles; Killyleagh & District Branch of the North of Ireland Family History Society.

Initiative; Seeconnell Community of South Down.

Lisburn Historical Society Journal.

Outline; West Belfast Historical Society.

Saintfield Heritage; Saintfield Heritage Society.

South Belfast Historical Society Journal.

Twelve Miles of Mourne; Mourne Local Studies Group.

Upper Ards Historical Society Journal.

Video:

Fermanagh Cultural Heritage: a Historical Journey; Breege McCusker;
    Necarne Educational Production, Irvinestown, Co Fermanagh.

Forthcoming:

Ongoing research on old country games and pastimes of Ireland and
Britain, linked to the Council of Europe's project 'Traditional Games
of Europe' (Committee for the Development of Sport: 'Sport for All'
initiative), by Andrew Steven ('Hillcrest', 5 Beech Hill Avenue,
Saintfield Road, Belfast BT8 4NS. Tel: 0232 702315) is expected to
result in two 1992 publications, as follows:

> A comparative study of old countryside games in Ireland, relating
> them to similar pastimes in Britain and continental Europe;
> An illustrated booklet to encourage the survival of old countryside
> games amongst young people.